THE INFORMED INVESTOR

HOW TO USE THE
MONEY MEDIA
TO IMPROVE
INVESTMENT
PERFORMANCE

RAY VICKER

PROBUS PUBLISHING COMPANY
Chicago, Illinois

Library of Congress Cataloging-in-Publication Data

Vicker, Ray.
    The informed investor : how to use the money media to improve investment performance / Ray Vicker.
      p.   cm.
    Includes bibliographical references and index.
    ISBN 1-55738-134-8 : $18.95
      1. Investments—Information services—United States.
2. Television broadcasting of news—United States. 3. Journalism.
Commercial—United States.   I. Title.
HG4515.9.V53   1990
322.6—dc20

                                      90-44993
                                          CIP

Printed in the United States of America

BC

1 2 3 4 5 6 7 8 9 0

Contents

Preface

When investing, it seems axiomatic that one must seek all available information about the investment before parting with cash. The more you can transform yourself into a law-abiding market insider, the better your chances for profit.

But worthwhile moneymaking information isn't always readily apparent or all investors would be multimillionaires. The sheer volume of financial data in today's money media may confuse rather than enlighten. On the same day, you may hear that the stock market will skyrocket, plummet or meander sideways. You definitely need help to act upon such data, but from where? How can you separate money information nuggets from the information avalanche?

The media shows you the way if you know where to look. I wrote *The Informed Investor* to help you in that search. Investing consists essentially of acquiring information, then reacting to it. You can become a market insider without breaking any laws if you heed the book's suggestions.

The chapters that follow survey that media—the TV financial shows, publications like *The Wall Street Journal* and *Investors Daily*, newspaper business sections, over forty financial magazines, several hundred investment letters, uncounted stock brokerage publications and many other sources, from government bulletins to statistical services.

The book identifies profitable sources and shows you how to profit from them. No such guide can tell everybody where to invest; this one explains how to improve information channels to sharpen personal financial decisions.

In writing this book, I drew upon more than thirty-six years of experience in financial journalism, most of that time with *The Wall Street Journal.* In those years I encountered many American and foreign financial and investment giants, listened to their stories and analyzed their investing strategies. I noted that the successful drew information from the money media even as they contributed to the news distributed by its organs. They made themselves "insiders," and with some exceptions they lived within the law when doing so. You will gain merely by copying their methods of operations, if you do nothing else.

In this book, I address people who invest for the long term rather than speculators eager for the allegedly quick profit. Patience pays. You can grow rich gradually as well as through a bonanza, but the former carries much less risk than the latter.

I cite informational pitfalls lying amid the piles of data. Successful investors not only utilize information to make money, they use it to avoid losing capital as well. In investing, you win some and lose some. You succeed by minimizing the losers while maximizing the winners.

An appendix provides the addresses of publications, services and offices mentioned in the text should you wish to contact them. The name of a source means little if you can't reach it quickly.

I owe much to people who helped me either directly in the writing of this book, or through information provided over the years when dealing with them as a reporter or editor. Foremost in that group comes my wife, Margaret, who assisted in my research, edited much material and provided a steadying hand whenever barriers seemed insurmountable. Helpful media friends are so numerous that I must thank them *en masse,* lest any colleague be overlooked.

Ray Vicker

Chapter 1

You, Too, Can Be An Insider

INSIDER SOURCES FOR PROFIT

Ivan Boesky manipulated inside information illegally in the process of building a personal fortune of some $250 million, claims the Federal Government. That's enough to make anybody take notice.

Most investors wish that inside information would gravitate toward them, without leaving any tell-tale trail of paper to excite the Securities and Exchange Commission (SEC). Maybe not $250 million worth. Just a little here, a little there and then some atop that.

Actually, you can acquire much valuable information legally, if you open your mind to the media volume already flowing around you. You violate no law, for the data is available to all. But not everyone pays attention to it. Not everyone knows how to interpret it. Learning how gives you an advantage.

Such information will not match data available to the crooked trader or unscrupulous corporate executive. But you can improve your profit possibilities enormously, without angering the SEC.

The information-spouting media includes the financial press, television programs like *Wall Street Week*, radio shows, government reports and statistics, investment advisory letters, broker publications and more. For twenty-four hours a day, seven days a week, the "money media" distributes data which can transform you into an investing insider if you learn how to tap the flow.

1

All investing involves obtaining information, then acting upon it. The more inside it can be without abusing SEC guidelines, the better for you.

The SEC itself offers much investor information, ranging from detailed company studies to a pamphlet for novices, *What Every Investor Should Know*.

Brokerage offices freely dispense helpful publications, too. Take pollution control, a hot investing area today, for example. Smith Barney, Harris Upham & Co., the brokers, recently published an analysis of this field. With the report, you could lecture on the topic, or pick some profitable investments.

If bonds interest you, Merrill Lynch freely distributes *The Bond Book*. In twenty pages, it explains the various kinds of bonds, their rating systems and much more. Brokers overwhelm you with studies like this, many larded with sales promotion, most containing some factual information of worth. Look for those nuggets which may prove profitable to you.

COLLECT DATA FOR PROFIT

Once you dig for data, you find veins of it running in all directions. Smart investors start as investment information collectors. Then their profit accumulation begins.

You can't ignore financial information just because you aren't in the stock market at this time, either. If you intend buying a house, the level of interest rates determines your monthly payments. To vacation in Europe, you should know dollar exchange rates. The health of your bank affects your savings even if it is insured for up to $100,000. If you have children headed for college, it may take sharp financial planning to get them there.

Nearly everybody requires some personal finance information at various times all through life. So apply yourself—you can glean gold from the data motherlode once you realize how much it may enrich your pocketbook.

INFORMATION TYPES

For investors, data falls into two basic types: fundamental and technical. You may benefit from both. Novice investors probably benefit more from the first than the second. Still, they should be aware of what technicians offer.

Fundamental Data

This involves almost any news about a particular company or about the market. This might include company sales levels, profit trends, current earnings, dividend payments, debt, management moves, and so on.

A simple report of employee layoffs could signal a company slowdown. A hiring announcement might indicate good prospects. Such information moves stock prices. When Seagate Technology, a California high-tech company, reported unexpectedly lower earnings in June, 1988, its stock dived more than 40 percent. Wise investors who followed insider stock trading of company executives probably had already sold shares. Less informed share holders probably had not.

"Insiders" Explained

In market language, all corporate executives are "insiders" since their positions provide knowledge of their companies which ordinary investors can't acquire easily. They may buy or sell shares of their own companies. But the SEC requires them to file notices of such trading and it releases the data to the public. Ostensibly, by focusing light upon insider buys and sells, outsiders can share some of the edge possessed by corporate executives.

In the Seagate case, an executive dumped a third of his company holdings weeks before the report. That news was readily available for investors who knew where to find it. Such selling by a company insider sometimes forebodes troubles. Informed investors study such buying or selling and often react to it. They make themselves legitimate insiders in order to sharpen their own investing edge. They watch for unusual activity, such as more selling than normal or heavy purchases by insiders who should know the company's outlook better than any outsider. Typically, insiders sell twice as often as they buy. If the buyer percentage rises, that is considered bullish for the stock, and vice versa.

Heavy insider buying among many companies usually forecasts a stock market rally, say the experts. Conversely, if the number of insider sellers rises from par, professionals read that as a bearish development.

If this sounds complicated, do not despair. The money media offers you the data, usually with all the interpretations necessary for ascertaining the meaning of any trading. *The Wall Street Journal* reports insider purchases and sales at least once a week. Newsletters such as *Insiders' Chronicle, Vickers Weekly Insider Report, The Insiders* and others devote space to trading by key officials within companies.

Invest/Net, Inc., a North Miami, Florida, investment advisor, distributes a weekly report to newspapers. You might see it in your daily paper. Public libraries contain helpful investing publications such as *Value Line Investment Survey*, the *New York Times* or *Barron's* which may also analyze insider trading.

John S. Reed, chairman and chief executive officer of Citicorp., certainly endorsed his company through insider trading in late 1988. He purchased 100,000 shares of Citicorp at $25 per share, a $2,500,000 bet on the big bank's future.

Moreover, he bought his stock in the open market. Usually, executives buy shares through their company's option plan at a reduced price. Professionals view insider buying at market prices through brokers as a double endorsement for a company.

Should you buy or sell a stock based upon insiders trading alone? Not necessarily. Combine that information with other data, then formulate your buy or sell strategy.

Applying Fundamental Data

Worthwhile investment information comes from many directions because so many things affect shares. A share might rise simply because a respected stock trader favors it. So smart investors follow the share trading of a known super stock-picker like Warren Buffett, chief of Berkshire Hathaway, Inc. Why not? Over twenty years, he earned a return of 20 percent a year for the company's shareholders. Berkshire's stock stood at $19.46 when Buffett took control in 1965. In 1990 it peaked at $8,900.

Be a copycat yourself, and watch some of those top investors to reap profits of your own. You can't, of course, phone and ask Buffett what he is buying. You depend upon other sources— *Barron's*, the weekly tabloid, being one. Floyd Norris, then the writer of that publication's "The Trader" column, snooped among official records in states where Buffett controlled several insurance firms. Amid documents which few people outside the industry read, he did indeed find evidence of Buffett's trades.

You might have benefited from the subsequent story had you read *Barron's*. (Norris now digs for the *New York Times*, as writer of the "Market Place" column, which appears five times a week.)

Technical Information

Fundamental information means little to market technicians. These investors cull information from charts of market price trends, the volume of shares traded, sentiment statistics (number of traders who are bullish and bearish on the stock market) and other indicators.

The statistical data of an individual market technician may be public. Methods of interpreting it may be proprietary, developed through painstaking study. Technicians guard formulas like a gold prospector guards the only map to a rich mine. However, you might be able to subscribe to the technician's advisory letter or service and benefit from his data without much further effort on your part.

Joseph Granville, a noted market technician, long contended that he possessed the ultimate formula for predicting stock market advances and declines. He showed less conviction after persuading most of his investment letter subscribers to sell everything just before a spectacular market climb.

Probabilities, Not Certainties

Even an expert makes mistakes, which isn't much consolation should you suffer from one. Technicians in fact often *do* predict market turns. In investing, you deal with probabilities, not certainties. The more information you collect, the higher your probabilities for success.

British-born Adrian Day, publisher of the monthly *Investment Analyst*, says in an investing perspective: "Estimating the future is a matter of probabilities. That's not as exciting as dramatic forecasts, but ultimately is of more value."

So investors face an endless task of gathering and digesting financial information, often available for free, sometimes for a fee. So much exists that one must learn what to absorb and what to ignore. However, the increased cash inflow sweetens such labor.

THE MONEY MEDIA

Sources comprising the money media range from *Business Week* magazine to investment letters like the *Zweig Forecast*, and from *Forbes* Magazine to pamphlets available for free in brokerage offices.

Companies readily distribute annual reports to present or would-be stockholders. Many supply their 10K reports, studies overlooked by average investors. Companies, by law, file these annually (10Ks) and quarterly (10Qs) with the SEC. Corporate annual reports often contain much fluff. The SEC, however, demands concrete details of operations in these filings.

The Book World

Financial tomes roll steadily from printing presses. Bookstores and libraries feature shelves of them. Serious investors benefit from the books published by the New York Institute of Finance. These include *The NYIF Guide to Investing, The Investor's Desk Reference, How the Stock Market Works* and *How the Bond Market Works.*

Dozens of other publishers, such as Probus Publishing, Dow Jones-Irwin, John Wiley & Son, Prentice-Hall, Bale Books, Enterprise Publishing and Financial Sourcebooks publish in this field. Send or call for their catalogs.

Helpful Markets

Exchanges provide free data. For booklets on foreign currency trading, contact the Philadelphia Stock Exchange (see the appendix for address). New York's Commodity Exchange distributes interesting material about dealing in gold and silver. Phone and ask, too, about their educational programs.

Seminars

Seminars generate additional information for investors. Financial experts explain how to plot strategies, pick products or manage portfolios. In Los Angeles, Charles and Kim Githler, conference promoters, conduct one such session on mutual funds in the Embassy Theatre. That venerable establishment, with its musty atmosphere and 1920's air, attracts a crowd even to this day. Attendees amble down its sloping aisles, sidle into red upholstered seats and listen like school children as speakers extol merits of fund investing and asset switching. They ask questions and scratch notes on pads. One hopes that they depart with numerous profit-making ideas. So may you at some future meetings.

Seminars cover every conceivable money topic. In June, 1989, Seminars International and *Lottery Magazine* even held a one-day affair in Fort Lauderdale, Florida, billed as: "The World's Greatest Lottery Conference." Attendees heard the Briton, Frank Honywill George (cq) and Dr. Darrel A. Dolph describe systems for beating lotteries.

Investment Letters

Hundreds of investment advisory letters serve investors. These suggest strategies, name hot stocks, warn of hazards and offer money advice. Letters vary in style and content. A few present copy in a folksy manner. Technical publications print many charts. Sometimes conservative dogma abounds. One costs $10,000 a year, but

most sell for $75 to $400 a year. Many aim at segments of markets—
foreign shares, for instance—or mutual fund investing. Others target all markets. Nearly all try to think for you.

"For $97.50 a year, I'll send you the same powerful stock picks
that Shearson Lehman Hutton or Drexel Burnham Lambert pay
$120,000 a year for," says a promotion from Brian W. Smith, Pub-
lisher, KCI Communications, Inc., which sells investment letters and
services. In 1989, the Newsletter Association awarded KCI's 86,000-
circulation letter, *Personal Finance*, first prize for editorial excellence
among financial letters.

This particular KCI promotion concerns *Innovest*, a computer service which screens 9,000 stocks daily and picks those considered
promising investments.

The Financial Press

A few years ago, newspapers usually shunned business news. Now,
even moderate-sized dailies contain business sections. America's
biggest daily is not a general newspaper; it is the two-million circulation *The Wall Street Journal*.

Over forty-five business and financial magazines crowd newsstands. You don't need a guide to tell you that *Financial World* or
Money focus upon investing.

Trade Journals

In your information searches, don't overlook trade publications, either. Savvy investors in bank and financial shares benefit from
reading the *American Banker*, as one example.

Serious gold bugs, those investors who believe gold is the financial salvation of mankind, probably read *The Northern Miner*. This
Toronto-based periodical provides readers with an unbiased picture
of gold mining companies and the industry.

Technical publications help, too. The newsletter, *Heap and Dump
Leaching*, sounds a bit too much like an engineering publication—
which it is—to appeal to most investors. Still, leaching advances in
recovery of gold from ore revolutionized the mining industry in

recent years. New gold mines surface around the world, thanks to this development.

Investors who bought stocks early in the lives of some of the new producers profited handsomely. They obtained information about the new process from trade magazines well before the news reached the general press. Then they quickly acted. This is the way legitimate inside information opens profit doors for you.

Trade publications exist in nearly every industry. A magazine for doctors might report a new painkiller. That alerts investors to a drug investing opportunity. An article in *Chemical Business* about a new plastic could benefit a company's stock. Gene splicing discoveries usually appear first in a science publication rather than in the daily press.

So it goes. Profit boosting information lies all around. The market pro notes everything that might benefit a portfolio. The investing amateur trips over inside information and misses its significance. Rise above the amateur level and the market rewards you well for it.

COMPUTERIZED INFORMATION

The computer, the modem and telephone technology create more areas for information distribution. *Dow Jones News/Retrieval*, CompuServe's *InvesText*, the *Source Information Network* and dozens of others provide reams of data to subscribers. Services provide fast access to information available to financial firms, banks, insurance companies and money managers.

A subscriber at home or in an office punches computer keys to connect with a network via telephone lines. A menu of choices appears on the computer monitor. These cover the databases offered. The customer selects the area of interest, uses other menus for investment reports and news items. With a printer, the client copies incoming information.

InvesText's database includes brokerage reports from twenty-six Wall Street firms, thirteen regional brokerage houses and twelve foreign investment companies. *Dow Jones* offers everything in the current *Wall Street Journal* and *Barron's*, plus data from back issues. It also sends price and volume information about markets and specific stocks, SEC 10K reports, *Japan Economic Daily* news, money market and foreign exchange information and much more. The service even offers the transcripts of the most recent Louis Rukeyser television program, *Wall Street Week*, to subscribers.

As stock markets grow more volatile, the need for accurate information becomes ever more important for investors. That data helps you decide what and when to buy, how to allocate funds among investments and when to sell.

INFORMATION BREEDS HUNCHES

Smart investors draw advice from many sources and couple data with hunches. Intuition stems from digesting the worthwhile information collected earlier.

With the right data, you can indeed beat the market. Rodney J. Miller, an athletic weightlifter and stock broker, has been doing that for years at Dean Witter's Walnut Creek, California, office. He recommended Dart Drugs to clients when it sold in the $5-$8 range. Subsequently, it went to $175 a share. You don't need many stock tips like that to grow rich.

In 1988, *Money* magazine named Miller as one of the nation's ten "All Pro" stock pickers. Appropriately enough, the license plate on his blue Mercedes sedan says: "STOK PKR."

The right information has turned others into "STOK PKRs," too. Proof of that lies in the careers of smart investors such as John Templeton, Peter Lynch, Charles Allmon, Warren E. Buffett and others of their calibre who consistently find market bargains.

AIMS OF THIS BOOK

Certainly it takes work to separate the informational grain from the chaff. This book aims to ease that task by identifying worthwhile sources in the money media and describing ways to tap them. It also identifies informational pitfalls hidden amid the mountains of data. An appendix provides addresses of publications, services and offices mentioned in the text should you wish to contact them.

Develop Cynicism

Information may answer many questions. It also should stimulate a degree of cynicism. You soon find that erroneous information exists along with worthy ideas. Even a saint may discover that allegedly inside information might be disastrous.

In 1431, Joan of Arc, the French saint, irritated the English when on the stand defending herself against charges of witch-craft. She shocked the court by declaring that the angels and saints in heaven speak French, not English. No Englishman visualizes a French-speaking Saint Peter at the Pearly Gates. Moreover, Joan couldn't explain how she had obtained this "inside information" about Paradise. Only the Devil could have provided such scandalous and patently false data to her, reasoned the court; so she must be a witch. That justified her burning at the stake, a sentence duly implemented.

Ask Questions

Today, misinformation probably won't be fatal, but it could cost you a fortune. So ask questions and more questions before accepting anything as gospel. But be specific with your queries. Don't be like the minister who once preached a sermon in Trinity Chapel to students at England's Oxford University. At a key point, carried away by sound of his own voice, he asked the bored young men a rhetorical question: "Would you, my dear young friends, like to be inside with the five wise virgins, or outside alone and in the dark with the five foolish ones?"

The question brought down the house (or, more figuratively, the ceiling of the chapel). Before making any financial deal, you must ask questions, too—but not those with obvious answers.

CASE HISTORY OF UNASKED QUESTIONS

The dramatic collapse in 1988 of share prices of Regina Co., the Rahway, New Jersey, vacuum cleaner maker, shows how wrong even market professionals sometimes can be. Regina went public in 1985 at a price of $5.25 (after allowing for stock splits). The pros loved the stock. Its price zoomed. Numerous security analysts and financial publications touted Regina as a "growth company," meaning its share price should go up and up.

Shearson Lehman Hutton added the company to its Growth Stocks Recommended List. The stock stood at $25.25 a share when one money manager termed it "a smart stock pick." That opinion was voiced at a *Barron's* Round Table conference.

The *OTC Review* quoted Regina's chairman lavishly. Other publications published like articles, and various brokerage houses urged clients to buy Regina's shares.

Regina unexpectedly announced a sharp downturn in sales and profits. That jarred the market and raised fears about the company's heavy debt burden. Share prices tumbled 59 percent.

Yet hints of trouble existed in earlier data, provided one studied it closely. That positive report in *OTC Review* did contain a cautionary note. After lauding the stock, the article said: "The dust ball under Regina's spotless sofa, however, is the company's growing debt level."

In analyzing this debacle, *The Wall Street Journal* said: "The Regina lesson may be that glowing stories about companies should be read more for the one or two lines of caution than for the positive comments."

A Moral To The Story

Don't believe everything you read. Use common sense in interpreting incoming information. If a company's debt load exceeds a third of its equity value, be careful. Any time interest rates rise, such a company might experience trouble carrying the load. You find debt information in a company's annual report. The *Value Line Survey* provides it, too, for 1,700 companies, along with much other data as does Moody's and Standard & Poor's.

In the spring and summer of 1988 when Regina rode the crest of its popularity, interest rates were rising. Your daily newspaper probably carried stories about the trend. So did every major business publication. Regina's investors ignored implications.

A little investigation at retailers also could have warned investors to dump the stock fast. This company produces vacuum cleaners, a product known to nearly everybody. What were dealers saying about Regina's models? Did you know anyone who purchased one? What did he or she say about the product?

Simple questions, yet many stock holders never ask them about a corporation whose shares they buy. From hindsight, less astute investors at Regina learned that product quality had slipped. Buyers were complaining about the vacuum cleaners. As news spread, sales plunged. That caused the profit drop noted in the ill-fated earnings announcement.

Bruised investors well might use the example of Regina to avoid investing at all. They might ask: Why be in a precarious and volatile stock market which shoots up and down unpredictably? Indeed, small investors often regard Wall Street as a dark avenue where they might get mugged financially.

A few decades ago, Everette DeGolyer, one of the world's great geologists, liked to tell oil prospectors: "Use all the best geology you can and all the best geophysics. But be sure to carry a rabbit's foot in your pocket." Should the same comment apply to searching for good stocks? Perhaps, if you are superstitious. But first tap the money media for all the investing information you can acquire. The intelligence you obtain won't guarantee 100 percent success. You may need a little bit of luck. However, such luck is more likely to occur if good information and sharp reasoning accompany the rabbit's foot.

With the right data, investors face favorable odds when investing. This is the way you grow rich.

Chapter 2

Gleaning Profit From Information

With all the financial information available, it is easy to become confused. One Friday, a money manager on Louis Rukeyser's *Wall Street Week* advocates extreme caution in the market. The following week another guest on the program recommends the purchase of so many stocks that you miss a few when trying to copy names.

So it goes. Sources on television or radio forecast market trends. Newspapers or magazines make estimates. Experts publish expectations in investment letters, while alleged savants expound them at seminars. Your broker too might offer an opinion (usually optimistic, since his or her pay depends upon sales).

MARKET EXPERTS DISAGREE

Answers often conflict: predictions claim the market is going Up! Down! Sideways!—take your pick. On any one day, varying predictions arrive. To compound the confusion, some university professors condemn all predictions. They claim it is a waste of time collecting market information, because markets move randomly.

Whom Can You Believe?

Diverse opinions create confusion. Are the market bears correct
with their gloom and doom worries? Or are the bulls right when
they claim we face the biggest boom of this century? And what
about this Ivy Tower contention which views the market like a
giant lottery, where luck determines everything?

HISTORY SUPPLIES ANSWERS

Records show that over decades the stock market climbs ever
higher. On a chart, the trend line peaks, falls into a canyon, then
rises to a higher peak. That repeats time and again to ever higher
summits.

"Ah, but that's because of steadily rising inflation," explain the
naysayers. Granted, the chart reflects some inflation. Look closely
and you see that the climb *outruns* inflation.

Upward Long-Term Trend

The Dow Jones Average of stocks certainly appeared low on October 19, 1987, when it fell 508 points to 1738.74. That low point far
exceeds the 1981 bottom of 824. On a long-term chart, the 1987
crash becomes a blip on an upward trend line.

Individual Shares Zoom

American Express sold for only $6.10 a share in 1980, when ad-
justed for splits. It started 1989 at $26.63. You could have purchased
Ford Motor Co. stock for as little as $4.10 a share in real terms in
1980. On January 3, 1989, you needed $50.50 to buy it.

Hundreds of companies experienced stock price rises of five
times or more in the last decade, considerably more than the inflation rate. Compaq Computer, a growth whiz with no stock listing

in 1980, sold for as low as $3.50 a share in 1984. It reached $101.50 in 1989. Other examples abound.

Certainly, nothing guarantees a repeat of like climbs in the future. All companies do not participate in the long-term market rise. But over time, chances of a noninflationary increase in stock market values far outweigh those for a decrease.

The Stock Payoff

Over decades stocks have paid 10 percent annually on average, says Merrill Lynch. That compares with about 3 percent in super-safe Treasury bonds. A dollar invested in Standard & Poor's 500 in 1925 swelled to $345 by 1988, reinvesting dividends.

Again, what about those Ivory Tower professors who claim that luck dominates markets?

THE EFFICIENT MARKET THEORY

Proponents of this theory smugly claim that stocks move randomly and unpredictably. Stock exchanges operate so efficiently that prices reflect all available information about shares, say they. In other words, if a stock you consider worth $100 a share sells for $50, your information errs. The efficient market alone set the correct price of $50, say the professors. Price changes in the future would be random.

These theorists claim that an investor selects better stocks with a dartboard than through patient analysis. So forget about study, chart reading, broker's tips, investment letters, watching Louis Ruykeyser on television or using other, far more arcane tools to predict future movements of shares.

What nonsense! Inefficiencies *do* exist in markets. Executives misjudge the worth of their companies. Misinformation exists. Sometimes professional speculators ignore certain stocks through laziness or misinterpretations. This environment creates buying opportunities for you; information steers you to them.

Dart Board Stock Picking

If you ever pick stocks using a dart board, first put certain names on the target, such as Abbott Laboratories, American Cyanamid, Coca-Cola, General Electric, Merck & Co., Proctor & Gamble, Quaker Oats, Royal Dutch Shell, Unilever, the Washington Post and William Wrigley Jr. Company.

You could be pretty sure that any investing system with a dart-board stock selector similar to the above would beat that of a college professor blindly using a page from *The Wall Street Journal's* daily market reports as the dart target.

Smith Barney, Harris Upham & Co., the brokerage firm, thinks so little of the Efficient Market Theory that it labels a continuing study of stocks as its "Inefficient Market Series." Each forty-eight-page report, published periodically, lists over a dozen companies which the firm regards as undervalued.

VALUE LINE'S DEFINITIVE ANSWER

Perhaps the best argument against the Efficient Market Theory comes from stock rankings maintained by Value Line Inc.'s Investment Survey. This is one of the oldest and biggest of this country's investment advisory services.

Each week *Value Line* names 100 shares which it feels should beat the market in the following year. Star shares may repeat week after week if their apparent worth holds firm. It also ranks another 1,600 shares in four other brackets of receding prospects for the twelve months ahead.

Value Line's *Record*

Group 1, the stars, not only consistently outperform lower ranked shares, but market averages as well. Suppose you had invested an equal dollar amount in each of the stocks of all five categories from best to worst from April, 1965 through 1988, reinvesting proceeds annually to keep funds in the same brackets.

Your Group 1 stocks would show a 2,388 percent gain versus a 227 percent rise in the New York Stock Exchange Composite. Stocks in the other categories would show increases of: 1,345 percent in Group 2; 603 percent in Group 3; 208 percent in Group 4; and 25 percent in Group 5. Not only does the system select winners, it names lemons as well.

Practitioners of the Efficient Market Theory offer only lame explanations of why *Value Line* possesses such a record if luck alone determines stock winners and losers.

Check the latest list in *Value Line* at your library, at your broker's office or at home through a subscription to the publication. While the *Survey's* long-term record merits applause, it does not beat stock market averages every single year. Few people, if any, do.

If you wish to learn more about the Efficient Market Theory, you might read Burton Malkiel's *A Random Walk Down Wall Street*, Fifth edition. The work, published by W.W. Norton, is available in hardcover. Malkiel, Dean of Yale University's School of Organization and Management, does present his case with clarity.

UNIVERSITY RESEARCH HELPS

Good studies also emerge from schools around the country. The American Association of Individual Investors monthly magazine, the *AAII Journal*, frequently publishes some of these. One, in the November 1989 issue, examined high yield (junk) bonds. The report, by Stanley Block, Professor of Finance at Texas Christian University, noted that this market has boomed from $24 billion in 1977 to $200 billion in 1989. Opportunities exist in that market for those willing to accept the risks, he wrote.

Nuggets From Research

Other university research shows: investors fare better by investing in shares of small companies rather than in those of corporate giants; returns from equities far outrun those from bonds over the long haul; investors who buy shares to hold awhile do better than those with a fast portfolio turnover; and diversification of a portfolio lowers risks, markedly.

Add this information to your investing arsenal!

OTHER WAYS TO BECOME RICH

Entrepreneurship

Stock investing doesn't suit everybody. Operating your own successful business beats passive stock investing by a wide margin. If you want to grow rich quickly, develop a good idea, obtain financing and become an entrepreneur. Once profits roll in, plow them into the business, depending upon an appropriate salary for your income.

Unassuming Sam Moore Walton, chairman of Wal-Mart Stores, Inc., testifies to that. Over a quarter of a century, he created America's most successful merchandising chain. Today, 200,000 workers call him "The Boss." Twelve hundred Wal-Mart stores enjoy nearly $16 billion in sales annually. Over seventy years of age, he still keeps a hand in operations.

If you meet him on the street near his Bentonville, Arkansas, headquarters, he probably won't look much different from a farmer in town in a pickup truck (which is what he drives). Modestly, he deprecates the fortune acquired from his successful business.

"Only paper," says he.

As an afterthought, he adds: "All I have is my pickup truck and my Wal-Mart stock."

That stock, worth a few cents per share when he launched his business, sold for $40 in mid-1989. The Walton family holdings now approach $9 billion.

Some paper!

Not many possess the technical competence, marketing ability, administrative skills and vision needed to succeed as an entrepreneur. Forty percent of small businesses fail in their first year. Only one in four survive through the first five years. Of the survivors, only an infinitesimal number mushroom into the Wal-Marts, the

Apple Computers or the Microsofts. That's why this country rewards good entrepreneurs so well.

The Collectibles Road

You hear of fortunes being made with a collectible—with Picasso drawings, baseball cards, precious stones, antique coins, rare stamps, Chinese ceramics or something else. Reports usually exaggerate. Rewards usually go to experts in particular fields. Without specialized knowledge, you buy at retail and sell at wholesale, never a good way to profit.

Allan S. Chait of the Ralph M. Chait Galleries in New York is one of the smartest dealers in the art business. He scoffs at the idea of amateurs profiting in it. Says he: "If you think you can come into *this* business and play in the same league as the major collectors, well, that sort of naivete is an invitation to financial disaster."

So how expert are you? Can you recognize a choice diamond, a valuable painting or an authentic Louis XIV chair on sight? Anybody can collect coins, stamps or whatever as a hobby, but the money makers know far more than the basics of their fields. Becoming a collectibles expert is much harder than teaching yourself the basics of personal finance.

Real Estate

In the past, real estate generated a lot of money for a lot of people, especially in the inflationary 1970s. Sure, you might match Donald Trump's early years—if you make a career of it. And that's just the point. To prosper in real estate, you proceed beyond passive investing. You acquire knowledge about construction, about remodeling, about foreclosures, about financing, about area prices, about marketing and about housing laws. Even that might not guarantee success, as Trump's stumble shows. Brilliant real estate operators fared miserably recently in Texas, Colorado, the Rust Belt and the Farm Belt. Now sources warn that real estate generally faces a crash akin to the stock market collapse of October 1987.

The forecast by Comstock Partners, Inc., a New York investment house, drew an avalanche of hate mail. Rising home prices outrank

apple pie as an American tradition among homeowners. To them, it
is heresy to even hint that the good years may be over in real estate.
You may disagree, too. Still, if you intend investing your money in
property, study the matter closely before doing so.

STOCKS STILL LEAD THE WAY

Adequate information and circumstances determine courses. Soon
you realize that stocks offer more opportunities for getting rich than
anything else for the average person with no talents for entrepreneurship, collectibles or real estate.

When you purchase stocks, you grab a financial bus which rides
up and down hill on the ever-climbing grade of a mountain so lofty
you never reach the summit. Remain on the bus through the valleys
and you rise higher than your point of departure. Sell in a dip and
you lose some of your investment.

Information Aids Decisions

What do you do when information seems confused? You search for
more information to reduce the uncertainty.

If you are a long-term investor, you hold strong shares bought earlier, knowing that markets likely will rise in the future. If you are
very worried, you invest in money funds. You also look to sources
for more of that "inside" information to guide your investing.

Patience Is Rewarded

Time favors you as an equity investor as you *patiently hold strong
stocks for as long as information favors them.* The quickly-in-and-
quickly-out trader is a speculator, not an investor. You need much
market knowledge to compete at that level.

Not everybody possesses the patience for successful equity investing. Bills become due. Family concerns may dictate liquidation.
Nerves wear thin. Many investors cannot operate on a long enough
cycle to benefit from the upward trend of the market.

But the shorter the time period for stock investments, the greater the risk for the investor. Heed that fact. Buy only what you expect to hold for awhile, unless you have so much money you can afford to gamble with some of it.

Investors should not depend upon any one source for information, no matter how good. Unforeseen factors may qualify even the best data. A digest of information from several sources produces better results than dependence upon one. Don't be bashful about watching and imitating market professionals, either.

AN INVESTING MODEL

Numerous models exist among successful stock pickers. Look at Mario Gabelli, top man at the money managing firm of Gamco Investors, Inc. He is a slender, enthusiastic individual who spouts facts with little prompting. You needn't question Mario too hard to obtain information—his comments just surface spontaneously, like a geyser erupting in boiling water.

His record justifies his volubility. Over the five years ending March 31, 1989, his equity investments posted a 29 percent annual profit gain, surpassing all money managers in the country tracked by CDA Investment Technologies. (This Rockland, Maryland, firm measures and compares earnings records of money managers.)

Barron's, the weekly tabloid of Dow Jones & Co., says: "Mario Gabelli is one of the great stock pickers of our time." It pays to listen when he speaks.

How Gabelli Picks Winners

Gabelli focuses upon specific stocks, not the market trend. He seeks value in stocks which sell at discounts because most investors ignore them. He prefers companies with little sales competition. He likes those which generate considerable cash, with underlying values which grow faster than inflation.

An example is Grief Bros., a shipping container company traded on the Midwest Stock Exchange. In 1988 its price hung around $37 a share, then climbed to $42.25 by January 1, 1989. Said Gabelli at the time: "They have about $6 a share in cash flow. They have $50 million in cash, which is about $4.50 a share. They have an over-funded pension plan. The company is worth about $67 a share."

He continually seeks new information about companies, in conversations, in documents cluttering his desk, in his perusal of financial publications. Has it paid off? Yes, says *Financial World*. The magazine says Gabelli personally earned "at least $6 million" in 1988, enough to place him among the 100 top earners on Wall Street. Moreover, he registered a 38 percent gain on the $1.6 billion portfolio managed by his firm.

A WINNING FORMULA

Successful investors preach buying low and selling high. That sounds trite when baldly stated; its like telling someone to pick a winner when they buy a lottery ticket.

Will Rogers, the legendary humorist, played with that theme when he said: "Don't gamble. Take all your savings and buy some good stock and hold it till it goes up. Then, sell it. If it don't go up, don't buy it."

Buying At Bottoms

Few investors recognize a market bottom until long after it has occurred. One of the extremely wealthy Rothschilds, however, did clarify when you might expect a bottom: "Buy when there's blood in the streets." He meant, of course, that you should buy when few others want to buy. That's how the rich grow ever richer.

Investors increase holdings of cash in unsettled times. They do not retire completely from markets. They know that downturns provide buying opportunities.

A smart investor can indeed beat the market with the right intelligence. *Changing Times*, the monthly magazine, terms information "the mother's milk of investing." This lactogenic description might not appeal to your broker, but it is a much friendlier description of brokers than others that have been heard.

Chapter 3

Gathering Data And Profits From Brokers

Woody Allen once said that a stockbroker is someone who takes your money and invests it until it is all gone. That doesn't say much for brokers, but by no means do all brokers fit this description.

America's retail brokers come in all sizes, shapes and sexes. Some help you profit in markets, and others do fit Allen's caricature. You can encounter people who know less than you do about markets, but you can also meet smart, honest professionals.

WHY USE A BROKER?

If you invest in stocks, you require a broker in most cases, though not in all. A good broker opens the door to a vast amount of stock market research which may broaden your investment horizons.

Major brokerage firms publish newsletters, stock reports, industry analyses, portfolio management tracts, computer screens of companies with attractive shares and a lot more which might prove profitable for you. Some material, of course, reeks of salesmanship. After all, brokers operate essentially as dealers of securities, and only marginally as financial advisors. The more they trade, the more money they make. Nevertheless, you can glean much useful information from such publications. Read them critically, accepting ideas just as you sometimes do from advertisements. Absorb the useful data; discard the sales spiels.

Broker Advice

Ask questions in your dealings with your broker. Remember, the squeaky wheel still gets the grease. A good securities person will describe the differences between a mutual fund and a trust, or between a zero coupon bond and a debenture. Such a broker helps you make money—big money sometimes; steady increments of it, more often.

DO YOU REALLY NEED A BROKER?

If you work for a company with an employee stock purchase plan (ESOP), you don't require a broker to purchase the available shares. (Check with fellow employees concerning the worth of the stock as an investment, though.)

You can reduce or skip dealing with a broker, too, if you concentrate your investing. Over 1,000 companies offer reinvestment plans which automatically reinvest dividends in new shares. Florida Progress, Pacific Gas & Electric and Koger Ptys., are only a few of the many companies with such plans.

Others offer shares directly to stockholders at discounts from the market price and without commissions. If you own no shares, you face an apparent wall. You may want to deal directly with the company, but you can't because you are not yet a shareholder. Catch 22? No! Go to a discount broker. Buy one share of the stock, or five or ten. That makes you a shareholder. Apply to the company for entry into its plan. Buy whatever you want. Some plans permit investments of up to $10,000 a month.

Finding Stocks Without Brokers

Write to the company of interest, care of "Shareholder Relations." Addresses can be found in the Moody's or Standard & Poor's references described in this chapter.

Finance publications sometimes name a few of these companies. *Moneypaper* (930 Mamaroneck Ave., Mamaroneck, NY, 10543) offers for small fees two lists: one of 914 dividend reinvestment plans; another of 350 direct investment plans. Try also *The Directory of Companies Offering Dividend Reinvestment Plans*, from Evergreen Enterprises (PO Box 763, Laurel, MD 20707-0763).

Don't purchase shares merely because you can buy them *sans* commission, though. Stick to good stocks which you would want under any circumstance.

Mutual Fund Purchases

Mutual fund investors need no broker. You can save money by purchasing fund shares directly from a fund, preferably one with a whole family of funds with switch privileges (see Chapter 10).

LOCATING A BROKER

If you invest substantial amounts of cash, sooner or later you probably will need a broker. Finding a good one is like locating a good medical doctor—not impossible, but not always easy, either.

References help. Ask friends, fellow workers, your bank. Investors like to discuss finance as long as questions don't get too personal. They brag about hot stock picks and will recommend helpful brokers.

Assistance comes from other sources, too. The Council of Better Business Bureaus offers a ten-page bulletin titled *Tips on Selecting a Stockbroker* (available for a small charge from the Council, Dept. 023, Washington, DC 20042-0023; send a self-addressed, stamped, business-size envelope).

Verifying Your Broker

You can obtain considerable information about your present or potential broker from the National Association of Securities Dealers (PO Box 9401, Gaithersburg, MD 20898; telephone 1-301/590-6500). Complete the group's information form and they send a summary of the education, employment history and disciplinary record (if any) of your proposed dealer.

Your state securities office usually can supply a similar background check. Call the North American Securities Administrators Association, 1-202/737-0900, to locate your state's office.

Barron's Finance and Investment Handbook, a 994-page reference guide, contains the addresses of state securities offices, plus lists of thousands of companies, of the world's stock exchanges, of scores of investment letters and much more. Most libraries have it and bookstores sell it.

Remember, a broker is essentially a salesperson. Be wary of hard-sell hucksters who glibly promise to double or triple your money overnight. Reliable brokers won't sell you something which doesn't fit your personality or risk tolerance.

TYPES OF BROKERS

Early on, decide which suits you: the discounters, like Charles Schwab & Co., Fidelity Brokerage Services, Inc., Olde Discount or Quick & Reilly, Inc.; or the full-service brokers, like Shearson Lehman Hutton, Prudential-Bache Securities Inc. or Merrill Lynch. Some investors use both—the discounter for simple trades, the full-service broker for transactions requiring more information.

Discounters

Discounters can be divided into two classes. Share discounters charge according to the number of shares traded; one hundred shares of $1 dollar stock costs you about the same commission as 100 shares of $10 stock. The value discounter bases fees on the value of the transaction, higher on the $1,000 transaction with the $10 stock than on the $100 deal with the $1 stock.

Full-service Firms

The full-service firm provides much more data about stocks and the markets than does the discounter. Moreover, other services they offer can be handy. Merrill Lynch's Cash Management Account, Dean Witter Reynolds' sweep program or Smith Barney's Vantage Account appeal to many investors. Accounts include check writing privileges, the quick deposit of idle funds into a money fund, use of credit cards and margin account borrowing (though not in IRAs). Information brochures on such programs will arrive frequently in the mail. Your broker will call with ideas. But you will need at least $20,000 to open the Cash Management Account and some of the others.

Full-service Commissions

Brokers at full-service firms do not talk much about their commissions. Be assured that they collect cuts on every buy or sell. This is fine if you obtain good service, but always be aware of the cost of the service and what it includes.

A $10,000 investment in United States Treasury bills yields $50 for the broker. A series of investments totaling $10,000 in options could pay him $2,000. So which do you think the broker recommends? Not necessarily options, if you have a quality broker who provides first-rate service. Nevertheless, given a choice between two paths, sometimes even the excellent broker may lean toward the more profitable product. Unfortunately, such products usually offer the most risk.

Limited partnerships and tax shelters carry steep brokerage commissions; 6-10 percent. Options are highly profitable for the broker, but very seldom for small investors. New-issue common stocks also fall in the high sales charges category. So do over-the-counter stocks and bond purchases in the secondary market.

Commissions on stocks depend on the item's selling price and the size of an order. Buys or sells usually cost 1 to 2.5 percent of the dollar cost of the transaction.

New bonds have commissions paid by the issuer, not you. You do pay the spread on secondary issues (those introduced earlier and now being resold). That might be 6-10 percent of the bond's $1,000 redemption price.

Bonds purchased at $920 each by the broker may be sold to you at prices ranging from $980 to $1,020 each. Sell those bonds before too long and the spread works in reverse—you might receive only $860 for the securities without any change in the market.

If you intend to buy $25,000 worth or more of bonds, brokers offer better deals. Small lot buyers do better in a bond fund.

Whatever you do, be very careful about surrendering power of attorney. Power of attorney allows the broker to buy or sell shares in your account without checking with you.

Never dash madly into any transaction involving money and never buy anything you don't understand. If a broker recommendation confuses you, seek written information for study at leisure. If the broker says, "Don't worry about it," you really should start worrying.

Don't select investments the way Mike Lansford, the field goal kicker for the Los Angeles Rams, boots his three-pointers. In one game, he kicked four field goals to score all the Rams' points in a 12-10 victory over the New Orleans Saints.

Asked later about it, he responded: "I just pick out a drunk behind the uprights, aim at him and hope it goes through." If you focus your investing aim on the financial equivalent of a grandstand drunk, you may end with a hangover.

Periodically, new closed end funds come to market, usually with heavy sales promotion. Few brokers warn that such funds usually decline drastically in value immediately after issue.

SEC data shows that prices of such new funds average 25 percent below the initial level after four months of trading. This comes after the 7 percent underwriting and sales fees paid by the investor.

Wise investors avoid original-issue closed ends. They wait and purchase them at discounts on the secondary market, with help of brokers who understand the value of providing service.

BENEFITING FROM A DISCOUNTER

You benefit from a discount broker through the much lower commissions you pay. Sometimes the savings can be as much as 70 percent compared to the full-service charges. That is especially true if you trade in commodities.

Commodity trading requires many deals to show profits. Stock investors usually buy or sell shares only three or four times a year. The commodities speculator trades twenty times a month, so commissions mount rapidly.

With a full-service broker, the commission for trading soybeans, pork bellies, financial futures and such ranges from $75 to $130 per contract. A discounter may charge less than $30 each.

Discount commodity brokers include E. David Stephens (1-800/421-0190 in New York, 516/248-6900 elsewhere); First American (1-800/621-4415); Transmarket Group (1-800/362-8117); Zaner and Co.; Futures Discount Group (1-800/872-6673); Jack Carl/312 Futures (1-800/621-3424); Lind-Waldock Co. (1-800/445-2000) and Ira Epstein & Co. (1-800/284-6000).

WHAT FULL SERVICE BROKERS OFFER

Major brokers justify their existence by trying to be financial planners, information centers and merchandisers for their clients. They offer enough money products to satisfy almost any sort of customer who pays for the services. That ranges from zero coupon bonds to options and from simple stock shares to certificates of deposit.

Tailored Products

Brokers tailor some products to meet special needs of clients. At the Hanover Square headquarters of Kidder Peabody in New York, executives praise the firm's special service for investors who receive lump-sum retirement payments from employers.

If you receive such a sum, you must decide whether to pay income taxes on the money through five-year or ten-year averaging.

You also may defer taxes through a rollover of the money into an IRA account within sixty days of collecting the total.

Deciding what to do may be the biggest financial decision of your life. A mistake costs you a bundle. Kidder Peabody applies Peat Marwick's computerized accounting to guide your decision.

Arcane Investments

A good broker helps with complicated investments such as puts and calls, short sales, commodity deals or more arcane investments. Speculators use put or call options to profit in either an up or down market. With a put, you promise to sell to the writer of the option (your broker) a fixed number of shares at a stated price within a specified period of time.

In effect, you gamble that the stock's price will drop before you must deliver the shares. The amount of that decline, less commission, would be your profit.

A call operates in reverse. You bet on a rise in a stock's price. Option trading requires constant surveillance of an account for best returns. So professionals do much better than individual investors. Records show that 90 percent of the people, usually novices, who buy puts and calls lose money.

Commodity Trading

Commodities offer profit potential, too, but again seldom for the amateur. Novices usually depend upon breaking news for "tips." But by the time a commodity development hits the network evening news, it is too late to make any money on it. Professionals already have the news and have acted. Their sources might be farmers in Iowa, cocoa buyers in Ghana, coffee roasters in Brazil or tin producers in Malaya. Each operator builds his own network of informants to get news first. With such pros occupying the other side of deals arranged by your broker, you face high odds trying to beat them.

Some Brokers Pick Stock Winners

Above all, you want good stock recommendations from any firm you utilize, picks like those of Legg Mason, Inc., the Baltimore brokerage firm. Every Thanksgiving it names a dozen stocks which it believes will outpace the market over the following twelve months. In nine of the ten years from 1979 through 1988, the Legg Mason list outperformed Standard & Poor's 500 stock index.

The record stands:

Year	Legg Mason (%)	S&P 500 (%)
1979	+34.09	+17.16
1980	+42.83	+41.19
1981	+19.04	- 5.29
1982	+56.83	+20.46
1983	+44.94	+26.61
1984	+29.88	+ 3.92
1985	+35.25	+26.18
1986	+26.75	+25.80
1987	- 4.03	+ 3.47
1988	+39.99	+13.99

BROKER LITERATURE

Firms liberally dispense market information, often focusing upon facets of investing which meet needs of people with money. A perusal of brokers' literature shows that asset allocation has become a catch phrase in investing today. That's a way of diversifying a portfolio between cash (money funds), bonds, stocks and other instruments. The latter might include real estate, gold, or foreign stocks.

Asset allocation fits an industry trend toward claiming that brokers operate as financial planners rather than as mere sales people. A good broker indeed may be almost a financial planner. A poor one might not even pass as a sales person.

A Company Prospectus

Brokerage houses prove especially useful when you want the prospectus of a company or a fund. A prospectus is a thick booklet, usually on onion-skin paper, with information about a company's new stock or bond issue or some proposition affecting the corporation's financial health. The SEC requires prospectus writers to reveal pitfalls of any deal, as well as reasons for it.

Merrill Lynch As Publisher

Merrill Lynch, a major brokerage firm, pours out market letters and brochures to its 5.5 million customers. *Retirement Planning* focuses on issues and developments for IRA holders and those preparing for retirement. Its monthly *CMA* letter recently advised readers to consolidate IRAs to save paperwork for themselves. Another article recommended United States treasury securities as "a strong foundation for a portfolio."

Additional information about treasury securities may be obtained free from Merrill Lynch by phoning 1-800/637-7455, ext. 8227, weekdays from 8:30 a.m. to midnight Eastern Time. Ask also for the brochure, *U.S. Treasury Securities: The Foundation of Your Investment Portfolio.*

The firm offers for free a special 40-page booklet for women, *You and Your Money*, a financial handbook. It contains many useful ideas (from which men too can profit) on personal finances.

Smith Barney Reports

This firm's monthly brochure, *Emerging Growth Stocks & Special Situations*, includes recent statistical data of over 100 such companies. The firm's *Topics* prints short reports of industries, media and entertainment, for instance, or aviation. *Market Interpretations* explains current stock market trends with technical analysis.

Shearson Lehman Hutton And Others

Shearson Lehman Hutton publishes a four-page news monthly, *The Serious Investor*. One issue named "uncommon values" among stocks. Dean Witter Reynolds distributes its educational *Money Talk* quarterly. In one issue, Marshall Loeb, managing editor, Fortune Magazine, clarified "the vast smorgasbord of choices" facing bond buyers. Stop at a Sears Financial Network desk in any Sears store for free booklets explaining how to analyze your net worth.

Financial firms offer far more publications than can be listed here. In fact, no one could read them all. Study them, but discard the sales pitches and the uninteresting offers. Seek hard information which might prove useful.

SECURITY ANALYSTS AND STRATEGIES

Collect studies of broker security analysts for profit, too. These well-paid employees research markets and companies. They profile stocks to help clients pick winners or to dump laggards. They recommend shares, outline portfolio management strategies as well.

Trading Range Strategy

A study by John Hoffman, manager of equity research at Smith Barney, recommends playing stock trading ranges for profit. At various times the Dow Jones Industrial Average fluctuates in a range of perhaps 300 to 400 points. Investor may make money by buying at the range low point and selling at the high, says Hoffman.

Dividend Strategy

Other analysts favor dividend payers. Dividends cannot be paid with accounting gimmick earnings. They require hard cash. Shoddy managements may not earn enough to pay stockholders anything. Well-managed companies register real profits and mail checks regularly to shareholders. Often their shares appreciate, too.

Stocks which increased cash dividends every year for the last ten years include: Allegheny Power, Bristol-Myers, Citicorp, Emerson Electric, First Interstate Bancorp, Humana, Johnson & Johnson and scores more.

Cleveland's Prescott, Ball & Turben, Inc., reports that investors who held the ten highest yielding stocks in the Dow Jones Industrial Index every year since 1972 averaged an 18 percent return.

When a stock in such a portfolio falls from the top list, you replace it with the newcomer in the top ten.

Don't, however, deify these researchers—nobody is infallible and some make poor recommendations. They search harder for stocks to buy rather than to sell. Still, if you read a report with some skepticism, you indeed may benefit from many of these studies.

RATING SECURITY ANALYSTS

The magazine *Institutional Investor* each year publishes its "All American Team" of security analysts, after polling 1,000 money managers concerning their favorites. In 100 pages the magazine explains its selections. It also rates brokerage houses according to the number of analysts placed on the All American Research Team. Merrill Lynch topped the poll for a decade, but ran fourth in 1988 behind Goldman Sachs (1), Drexel Burnham Lambert (2) and First Boston, Inc. (3).

Stars Among Analysts

Jerome Gitt, savings and loan stocks expert at Dean Witter Reynolds, has been on the All American Team for fourteen consecutive years. Jeffrey Klein of Kidder Peabody & Co. (pollution control shares) was a thirteen-time winner. So was Lee Seidler of Bear, Stearns & Co. (accounting).

Goldman, Sachs' Joseph Ellis has been an All American in retailing a dozen straight times. Dennis Leibowitz of Donaldson, Lufkin & Jenrette led the broadcasting field for eleven years in a row. To keep up with the All American Team, check each October's issue of *Institutional Investor* at a library, or buy a copy from the magazine.

INVESTING REFERENCES

Brokerage offices often contain reference books of worth to clients who don't make nuisances of themselves. Volumes include

Moody's and Standard & Poor's reference books, which contain stock reports, company histories, addresses and so on.

A client's welcome to peruse such material may depend upon the volume of business stemming from visits. Nobody likes freeloaders in a busy office. However, if your broker isn't helpful here, don't be upset. Most public libraries have such references, and they are worth pursuing.

Standard & Poor's

Standard & Poor's six-volume *Corporation Records* contains detailed descriptions of more than 12,000 public companies. Its twelve-volume *Stock Reports* analyzes 4,300 shares. *Industry Reports* studies 1,000 companies. *CreditWeek* covers the economy and interest rates and analyzes the quality of specific bond issues.

Moody's

Moody's *Bond Survey* covers the same ground as *CreditWeek*. Its *Manual and News Reports* analyzes 22,000 companies in eight volumes. Each volume examines a specific area, such as industrial, transportation, utilities, finance firms, and so on. *Industry Review* contains company news updated frequently in looseleaf binders.

Value Line

Many investors like *Value Line Investment Survey* (mentioned earlier) a twin-volume reference work you also may find at your broker or at a local library. The *Summary & Index* volume, with its more than 2,000 pages, contains thorough reports of over 1,700 companies. A second volume, *Selection & Opinion*, contains weekly market analysis along with specific recommendations for buys. Each issue features one hot stock rated as a superior buy.

Other References

You also glean much information from Gale Research's *Encyclopedia of Business Information Sources, The Dow Jones-Irwin Business and In-*

vestment Almanac, Dun and Bradstreet's Guide to Your Investments and
the Special Libraries Association's *Directory of Business and Financial
Services.*

PINK SHEETS

If none of these reference books provide information about a little-
traded stock, then the *Pink Sheets* might help. Ask your broker
about them. This market directory of Commerce Clearing House,
Inc.'s, National Quotation Bureau comes on 300 pink, onion-skin
pages each trading day. They list more than 20,000 companies
traded in the over-the-counter market.

A quarter of those stocks trade on the National Association of
Securities Dealers' Automated Quotation System (NASDAQ). The
remaining 15,000 provide grist for those pink sheets. Brokers term
these shares "penny stocks" because many do sell for pennies and
most aren't worth even that.

Some of these companies operate from tiny offices, with few people. They promote stock to attract capital for the factory they may
build after deciding what they might manufacture. Earnings may be
years in the future, if ever.

A few genuine stock gems do exist among the clutter. You must
hunt hard to locate them. You search even harder for potential
share sellers, with negotiations similar to those involved in buying
a house. One share might cost thousands of dollars.

Finding More Information

The National Quotation Bureau's semi-annual *National Stock Summary* provides some information about "The Pinks." *Special Situations Newsletter* offers an annual directory listing approximately
forty of the better Pink Sheet companies. For more information
about small stock investing, please refer to page 120 under FUN-
DAMENTAL STOCK APPLICATIONS.

Your broker might have data, too, but most brokers, except for
specialists in the field, despise "The Pinks" as nuisance stocks not

worth their time. If you insist, your broker probably can steer you to a specialist who may show you how to lose a lot of money.

The printed media provides much information for your investment program, too. Arthur Miller said, "A good newspaper is a nation talking to itself." A good financial newspaper or magazine talks to itself in the language of money. In the next chapter we listen in on the conversation.

Chapter 4

Financial Newspapers And Periodicals

DOW JONES AND *THE WALL STREET JOURNAL*

In his tastefully luxurious Lower Manhattan office, Warren H. Phillips, the chairman and chief executive officer of Dow Jones & Co., looks a bit like the actor Adolph Menjou playing a tycoon's role in a late-night television rerun. But Phillips' background better fits that of a character in Ben Hecht's "The Front Page."

Phillips climbed to the executive suite via the newsroom of *The Wall Street Journal*, the crown jewel in DJ's publishing empire. After fifteen years at the helm, he remains an editor at heart. He reads the *Journal* at morning coffee klatches in DJ's board room with a copy reader's eye for typos, unclear references and incomplete stories.

It surprised few that he lugged his typewriter with him when invited by the Chinese government to visit the country. Most news reporters tote their machines along even on vacations. On this occasion Phillips wrote an interesting story about China for the *Journal* and later co-edited a book about it.

DJ executives proudly aver that the *Journal* is a "journalists' newspaper." Indeed, the top DJ man has always reached the executive suite through the news ranks, never from other departments.

The paper also is "The Bible of Business," a must-read for investors who want to enlarge their holdings. It is not alone in that regard, though. Never have there been so many newspapers investigating ways for you and others to make money.

"One can say that good newspapers are almost always run by good newspaper people; they are almost never run by good bankers or good accountants," said the late C.K. McClatchy, editor and board chairman of the McClatchy Newspapers.

McClatchy, of course, was a newsman and journalists generally consider themselves an elite class. Still, look behind facades of such papers as the *New York Times,* the *Washington Post* or the *Los Angeles Times,* or publishing chains like Gannett or Knight-Ridder, and you will find ex-news reporters in executive suites. That is especially true in the financial news field.

Most business and financial reporters started their careers as green reporters, not as economic experts. Few of these novices could read a stock table or interpret a corporate annual report. With experience, the reporter becomes a financial expert. Very seldom does a career develop the other way, from accounting or money managing to writing and editing.

Nevertheless, skilled business and economic reporters may keep you informed about investments. They learn early how to write clearly and interestingly. If you intend plunking your hard-earned cash into any investment, you definitely want straight information, not advertising puffs or recondite financial gibberish.

You find such in *The Wall Street Journal,* which is why it draws over five million readers and nearly two million subscribers. Its famous Dow Jones Averages gauge markets. Investors closely follow its company earnings reports. Other publications frequently reprint its stories or quote from it. Its readers include America's movers and shakers. The average *Journal* household earns $146,300 a year; median income amounts to $85,800; net worth totals just over $1 million. Investments total $839,000.

One survey showed that 93.8 percent of *Journal* subscribers are college-educated. Males, at 88.2 percent, far outnumber female subscribers. Yet with so many women now entering business and finance, this distribution should change in the future.

The *Journal* is required reading in offices of brokerage firms, money managers, bankers and anybody else dealing with cash and corporate endeavors. You surely will find it useful if you do much investing, even if you do your reading at a library.

News Content

Each weekday, the paper presents three sections totaling up to 84 pages of business, financial, economic, political, international and general news along with three pages of editorial and entertainment copy.

Stories in the paper read easily, sometimes sprightly, following precepts developed by the late Barney Kilgore, the paper's guiding light from 1941 to 1967. He continually stressed that dull, complicated stories don't belong in a good business and financial newspaper.

At one *Journal* staff meeting in Bermuda, Kilgore discussed his writing ideas with this author. He was a relaxed man who seldom raised his voice to get attention. He said: "Stories should be clear enough to be understood by the housewife in Dubuque."

"That remark could be interpreted two ways," this author answered, though he knew well what the company's top man meant.

"I say it with respect for the intelligence of the housewife in Dubuque," Kilgore said. "Don't be so technical that only a technician understands your story. Don't write down to readers trying to be clear, either. Respect their intelligence."

The paper celebrated its 100th anniversary in 1989. In its history, it has won thirteen Pulitzer prizes and countless other honors. In 1988, reporters Daniel Hertzberg and James B. Stewart won a Pulitzer for coverage of the October 1987 stock market collapse. Walt Bogdanich won another in 1988 for specialized reporting.

Roger Cohen and Peter Truell won honors for Latin American debt stories. Alfred Malabre, economics editor, garnered the Columbia Business School's George S. Eccles Prize for excellence in economic writing with his book, *"Beyond Our Means."*

Robert L. Bartley, the paper's right-wing editorial chief, and Jude Wanniski, then associate editor, practically sold Supply Side Economics to the Reagan Administration. The thesis came from Arthur

B. Laffer, then a young University of Chicago economist. Bartley and Wanniski extolled its merits in the *Journal*.

However, the paper does not claim to be infallible. It currently faces stiff competition. It sometimes makes mistakes, which it acknowledges. And it would rather forget that in 1984 a reporter on its "Abreast of the Market" column leaked information in advance of publication to a stockbroker. That newsman, R. Foster Winans, departed in disgrace, was convicted of fraud and drew an 18-month jail sentence. So much inside information reaches the *Journal* that perhaps it was inevitable for abuses to develop.

Today, the Journal zealously emphasizes its long-established employee strictures against profiting from reporting or against leaking information prior to publication.

One three-and-a-half page memo on this subject from Ed Cony, then executive editor, warned: "It is not enough that everyone be incorruptible and act with honest motives. It is equally important to use good judgement and to conduct outside activities so that no one, our editors, an SEC investigator, or a political critic of the company, has any grounds for even raising the suspicion that you misused your position with the company."

Few people outside the news field realize the temptations offered to financial reporters for their "cooperation." It might be only a luncheon at a posh restaurant offered for a hopeful peak at a future story. It could be a gift at Christmas, or any time. It could be like the proposition made to a *Journal* reporter in Tokyo by a Colorado real estate executive.

This occurred in Spring of 1988 when Japanese investors appeared to be "buying up America." A real estate executive from Colorado correctly surmised that anybody working in Japan for the *Journal* might possess leads to Japanese investments. He offered a deal to the reporter: "In exchange for your help in locating these [Japanese] investors," he wrote, "I am willing to pay you a finder's fee of 10 percent of my commission for anyone who has been sent to me by you and a deal is consummated. On large purchases this could mean to you $20,000 and up. If you would like, any fees paid would be kept confidential from your employer whereas not to jeopardize your current position."

The reporter dispatched the letter to the home office in New York for a response. Norman Pearlstine, the paper's managing editor, sent this answer to the executive: "As you no doubt understand, as evidenced by your suggestion that payoffs be kept confidential from us," he wrote, "any *Wall Street Journal* employee would be violating our Conflict of Interest Policy by accepting your offer of a commission for help in locating Japanese investors for your real estate projects . . . Should we ever do a story on the sleazy, unscrupulous lengths U.S. real estate promoters will go to in seeking Japanese capital, I would certainly delight in using your letter (to Tokyo) as a prime example."

The Colorado real estate executive did not reply.

The Journal *Format*

The severe six-column format of the front page of the *Journal* may discourage readers the first time they encounter it. Like many things in life, the *Journal* is an acquired taste. The length of its front-page stories deters some—you probably can absorb a dozen pieces in *USA Today* before finishing one of the *Journal's* leders!

The staff on the paper terms the heavyweight stories on the right- and left-hand columns of page one as "leders," pronounced "leaders." They call the shorter, lighter center column front-page story "the A head." The short, often humorous piece in the lower-left hand corner of "The Marketplace" section's front page is known as "the orphan." That name originated in the early days of the *Journal's* second section. When editors didn't know where to place a short, light story not in harmony with the general run of business stories, they plunked it into the lower left-hand slot. Readers liked a bit of humor there, and the orphan found a home.

However, there hasn't been laughter at Dow Jones in recent times. Competing new business publications hit the *Journal's* circulation and advertising. For the first time in decades, DJ's earnings dropped. The *Journal* added new features, packed more information into its stocks tables, expanded graphic and visual displays, shook up the staff and honed its already sharp editing. Now its "Money & Investing" section aims directly at present or potential investors who hope to garner profit ideas from the *Journal's* pages. Here you find latest stock tables from the New York Stock Exchange, the American Stock Exchange and the National Association of Securities Dealers (NASDAQ) trading network, plus listings of numerous over-the-counter shares unregistered with NASDAQ.

Charts on columns 1 and 2 on the first page of this section visually illustrate such things as bond yields over the past eighteen months, the standing of the dollar against a packet of fifteen currencies, price trends of commodities and an "Investment Insight" table which analyzes various aspects of share trading.

THE DOW JONES INDUSTRIAL AVERAGE

A chart shows the constantly updated eighteen-month record of the index. The latest figure is the key statistic noted when a media source reports the rise or fall of the DJ Average. That tabulation predates the paper. Charles Henry Dow, a tall, courtly stock analyst, launched a hand-delivered Wall Street bulletin service in 1882, with Edward Jones and Charles Milford Bergstresser. The latter's name unbalanced the letterhead—so the founders reasoned. The venture therefore began as Dow Jones & Co.

Birth Of The Index

In November 1883, a compilation of the day's bulletins became the *Customers' Afternoon News Letter*. In 1884, DJ devised its first stock market index, an average of the closing share prices of ten railroads and two industrial companies. Dow surmised that these stocks significantly affected market trends. Wall Streeters liked the index. It became a fixture when the *Journal* emerged July 8, 1889 from the afternoon letter.

Over the years, editors revised and expanded indices to cover transportation and utilities as well as industrial shares. The latter compilation, the most quoted, now combines price actions of thirty major companies on the New York Stock Exchange.

It isn't perfect. The Standard & Poor's Index of 500 stocks or the NYSE's own compilation present better pictures of the market trend. So does the Wilshire 5000 Index, which covers 5,000 stocks weighted by their capitalization. But the long history of the DJ

Index provides a record which others can't match for long-term comparisons.

Charles Stabler, the retired *Journal* executive long responsible for the DJ Index, admits its flaws. But, he says, he rejects "tinkering with a barometer that's been useful over the years. I haven't been able to see how to correct it without losing continuity, which is one of the strengths of the Dow. How does the Dow compare today, with the figure on a specific date in 1962 or 1957 or whenever? With the DJ average, you can make the comparison," says he.

Two other indexes watched closely by Wall Street should be on your list, too, if you trade in small or medium-sized firms. They are the American Stock Exchange Market Value Index and the NASDAQ Over-the-Counter Composite Index. These show what investors think of those companies either too small for the NYSE or those which do not want a Big Board listing.

If the *Journal's* extensive business coverage confuses you despite its efforts to clarify financial news, help exists in *The Dow Jones-Irwin Guide to Using The Wall Street Journal* (Dow Jones-Irwin, 1818 Ridge Rd., Homewood, IL 60430). Written by Michael B. Lehmann, the work explains how to interpret the paper's economic and business information.

BARRON'S AND THE DOW JONES EMPIRE

Dow Jones possesses a whole stable of publications and news services beside the *Journal*. *American Demographics* interprets U.S. Census and other population data. *The Dow Jones News Service* feeds financial data over several thousand news tickers to brokers and businesses. If you have a computer, *Dow Jones News/Retrieval* can provide you with a wealth of investing information for a fee.

Barron's, a DJ weekly, reached a circulation of 250,000 in September, 1990. The tabloid appeals to market professionals. It covers investing strategies, promising stocks, important developments and such. Alan Abelson, its waggish editor, pokes fun at many of the shibboleths of Wall Street in his regular column. He also unmasks unscrupulous companies which overpromote their stocks.

Every quarter *Barron's* reports the mutual fund performances of 2,324 funds in the preceding three-month period. Statistics come from Lipper Analytical Services.

Barron's *Round Tables*

Frequently the publication quizzes prominent money managers, singly or in groups. Questions concern market trends, current buy-sell strategies and specific shares worth buying. *Barron's* tapes events and reports on them in question and answer form.

Often, Managing Editor Kathryn M. Welling moderates sessions, nimbly jousting with investors who deal in thousand-plus share blocks. She ably proves that finance is not an exclusively male domain.

"The Big Ten"

This high-powered affair, conducted every January, analyzes the outlook for the new year. That held on January 16, 1989, attracted ten top money managers to a lower Manhattan conference room. The group included Peter Lynch, the prematurely gray and now retired manager of the huge Magellan Fund and a buy-and-hold-awhile investor.

"Bristol-Myers has been a great stock," he said. "And Merck has been a great stock, and Melville Corp. If the Dow today were 400 or 700, you'd still have done well in Melville over the past 15 years."

But where would Melville be if the Dow were 400 today?, he was asked.

"It wouldn't be as high as it is now," Lynch admitted. "But, instead of being up fifteen-fold, it might be up fivefold. It still would be better than having your money in a bank."

Paul Tudor Jones II, 34-year old market trader from Tudor Investment Corp., noted pessimistic patterns on his charts and showed caution toward the market. But he added something you should remember anytime somebody in the future equates a current market decline with that of 1929, the precursor of the Great Depression of the 1930s: "In 1929, the dollar value of the United States stock market was almost 175 percent of the Gross National Product.

Today, it is 50 percent, and in many European countries, it is 20 percent. Stock markets are not as closely hinged to macroeconomic forces as in 1929."

Such nuggets abound when ten high-powered money men gather around a table. Mario Gabelli, chief investment officer of Gamco Investors, presented his bit of gold when recommending the auto-parts group if the economy slows. Says he: "There are about 120 million cars on the road and the industry is getting older, the gray-ing of the car population. Over 43 percent of the cars are over eight years old, versus about 33 percent in 1980."

Which specific stocks did he like at the time? "Genuine Parts, the Allen Group, Federal Mogul, Wynn's International and Champion Spark Plug," he stated.

Oscar S. Schafer, a general partner in Cumberland Associates, saw possibilities in troubled utilities such as Gulf States Utilities and Idaho Power, and liked paper and drug companies.

John Neff, portfolio manager of the Windsor Fund, usually out-performs the market. That day he favored Citibank, Bankers Trust, Ford Motor Company and a closed end fund under his manage-ment, Gemini II. Investors may earn 16.4 percent annually in this fund up to 1997, he said.

Michael Price, president of Mutual Shares Corp., showed little en-thusiasm for the market. But he liked a few depressed stocks trad-ing at below their breakup values. Among them: Amax Inc., Bass Breweries (a United Kingdom company) and Adolph Coors.

Ron Baron, who heads Baron Capital Inc., quickly outlined his strategy: "I try to concentrate on companies that are growing fast, that are selling at big discounts, that are asset values, and I focus on a few industries," he said.

Felix W. Zulauf, a director of Clariden Bank, Zurich, Switzerland, brought the European Continental perspective. Like most of the "gnomes of Zurich," he is cautious and favors bonds of five years or less maturity. But he saw oil prices strengthening, which should help the industry. He also liked Fluor, a heavy construction com-pany in petroleum.

Archie MacAllaster, who heads MacAllaster, Pitfield MacKay, Inc., reached to Norway to select Norsk Hydro as a stock pick.

Closer to home, he liked Arco Chemical as "a very cheap stock," the Bull & Bear Group and Hibernia Corp.

James B. Rogers Jr., a successful private investor who teaches finance at Columbia University almost as a hobby, forecast a steady market decline for the next couple of years. He liked Oakwood Homes' 7.5 percent bond of 2001, which redeems 5 percent of the bonds per year at par while paying 14 percent at the 68 price. He viewed this as a deal that couldn't lose. If lucky in the redemption queue, the investor collects $1,000 on every $680 investment. An unredeemed bond pays 14 percent annually.

The meeting lasted for eight lively hours and provided scores of buy recommendations together with explanations of the market strategies being followed by these experts. Tapes of these sessions filled long columns in *Barron's* over three issues. Letters to the editor subsequently showed that readers avidly follow such stories. (Stocks recommendations in a book may be long outdated by the time readers catch up with them, but investors may profit by noting the market thinking of the experts.)

Each week, *Barron's* devotes half of its 140-160 pages to statistics. You find weekly price lists of twenty-seven markets, ranging from Adjustable Rate Mortgage Base Rates to Variable Annuities. The pages also include thirty-four market indicators, twenty stock indexes and nine statistical compilations such as the book value of shares in the DJ Industrials or the stock/bond yield gap.

INVESTOR'S DAILY

Market professionals also follow another publication which contains numerous statistics of use in planning market strategies, *Investor's Daily*, the Los Angeles-based publication which calls itself "America's Business Newspaper."

William J. O'Neil, 57, founded the paper in 1984 as direct competition with *The Wall Street Journal*. It was a bold move. Nobody else has been willing to face the two-million circulation *WSJ* head-on with a business daily. The *Journal* does encounter much competition, but it comes from financial and business magazines, investment letters and business sections of general newspapers.

Even Rupert Murdoch, the Australian-born media tycoon, declined to challenge the *Journal*. Although he did express an interest in publishing a business daily. Nothing came of it.

O'Neil was an immensely successful stockbroker in Los Angeles. He made enough money from personal investments to purchase a seat on the New York Stock Exchange in 1963. In that year, he founded William O'Neil & Co., an investment research firm that big investors rate very highly. Nearly 600 of them pay as much as $100,000 a year to tap the firm's comprehensive stock database.

A second firm, O'Neil Data Systems, publishes industrial catalogues. Those companies provided the bankroll for the start-up. So O'Neil already possessed numerous weapons when he launched his business newspaper.

He needed them. He poured over $50 million into the operation, and probably hasn't made a profit yet. But, from scratch, he built a circulation of over 105,000, remarkable for the time period.

O'Neil's Investing Strategy

The paper reflects O'Neil's investing philosophy, which he claims has earned him a 40 percent annual return over the last ten years. He believes that a stock with expanding earnings and market momentum (the pace at which it is rising) rates higher than does one with low price/earnings ratios.

"The best time to buy is when a stock is making a new high in price after undergoing a price correction or consolidation," says he. "The best stocks are never selling at the bottom; they are usually selling near their highs."

That theory clashes with a lot of what passes for conventional wisdom on Wall Street—the buy-low-sell-high dictum, for example. Buy-high-sell-high raises eyebrows among some professionals.

Few publications present as sharply focused an investing philosophy as does *Investor's Daily*. In fact, most newspapers and magazines don't have any. Editors feel that they must remain objective in the presentation of data. Readers, then, formulate their own opinions and strategies.

Not so with *Investor's Daily*. It offers "An Audio Guide to Investor's Daily" with every new subscription. It tells the subscriber how to handle the information obtainable from the paper to achieve investing profits. Subsequently, subscribers find that stories and statistics focus upon that same general theme.

The stock tables presented differ sharply from those encountered elsewhere, too. The paper uses boldface for every stock that makes a new high or is up a point or more for the day. It underlines stocks declining to new lows or down a point or more.

It ranks all stocks on a scale from 0 to 99 according to the earnings growth of each company measured against all other publicly traded ones. A stock showing a rank of 90, for instance, tells you the company's earnings are in the top 10 percent of the more than 6,000 companies tracked each day by *Investor's Daily*.

Relative price strength compares the price performance of each stock over the last twelve months against all other listed stocks. A stock ranked at 80 on this scale has outperformed 80 percent of all listed shares. O'Neil likes charts and he obliges with ninety graphic displays in each issue, thirty of which involve shares hitting new highs or record volume the previous day.

The paper prints Psychological Market Indicators, statistics based on the crowd psychology of investors. These provide clues to market directions once you learn how to read them.

Three pages of bond statistics and news aim at fixed interest investors. Mutual fund rankings cover 1,000 offerings, with three high-rated funds in the Growth, Specialized and Income fields profiled each day. These reports help readers to select appropriate investment vehicles.

"Since three out of four stocks will slump in a bear market, you should avoid doing much buying then," says O'Neil. "To help you recognize critical turns in the general market more easily, we print full page-sized daily charts of key indexes."

OTHER FINANCIAL DAILIES & WEEKLIES

The Media General Financial Weekly, until recently, provided financial news and two dozen summaries of key investment letters to market professionals. Each eighty-page issue offered more current statistical data than is available in most other publications. But its market dwindled with the growing troubles at brokerage offices. In February 1990, it ceased publication of the paper and started providing data to subscribers via computers. Is this the shape of things to come in financial journalism? Not necessarily. Printed financial journalism is far from being dead. However, electronic distribution becomes an ever stronger competitor.

The Financial Times

This import from London now has gained a foothold for itself in the United States. Referred to as *The Fin Times* and "the pink sheet," it covers international, general, financial and business news. Here you'll read about mining in South Africa's gold fields, Zambia's Copper Belt, Australia's arid mining regions and elsewhere. Mideast oil gets broad coverage; so do world shipping and tropical commodities.

It reports in depth about corporations and their shares and about political and economic news affecting them. Stock, bond, option and other tables abound. It claims over a million readers in 155 countries.

It publishes more than 250 special surveys annually and distributes them to subscribers. These surveys address such issues as Corporate Communications, International Property, Biotechnology and Aerospace, along with geographic studies such as Arab Banking, Japanese Electronics or Canadian Finance and Investment.

The Financial Times also offers a lively arts and culture section, with handy reviews of plays, operas and concerts should you be travelling in London or on the Continent.

The Journal Of Commerce

This New York City-published daily competed with *The Wall Street Journal* as a key financial newspaper a half century ago. Now it focuses upon sections of the business world not covered in detail by other publications. Its beat includes maritime, commodities and trade news.

USA Today

This national publication has a broader content than do the financial papers. Still, among other things, the easy-to-read 1.6 million-circulation daily offers its readers a six- to twelve-page *Money* business section in every issue. This focuses upon personal finance topics, using what journalists term a "circus make-up"—various typefaces for headlines, wide and narrow columns on the same page, numerous graphs and drawings.

Color brightens the entire newspaper. Stories aim at helping the investor as well as reporting the news. One story about the RJR Nabisco takeover battle discusses developments in objective news style. Below it appeared a subjective story headed "Shareholders' Choice: Hold or Sell Now." This piece analyzed what the battle meant to the average shareholder.

The *Money* section tightly summarizes the day's major business and financial news in its "Moneyline" column on the left side of the section's page one. Just below it is "USA Snapshots," a visual, cartoon-illustrated presentation of some statistic or fact which shapes your finances.

"Fewer take IRA tax break," read one headline. A drawing of a piggy bank with a graph showed that 15.3 percent of taxpayers deducted for an IRA in 1984, but only 7 percent in 1988. "Homing in on our mortgages," read the headline on another day. Color drawings of different family combinations show what homebuyers say they can afford to pay each month for a home. The average First Time Buyer reported a $708 monthly figure. The Move-up Buyer can afford $897. The Empty Nester pays $631 a month, while the typical Retiree spends $720.

Stock price quotations fill two-and-a-quarter pages. Readers' questions, with the paper's answers, occupy another column inside, every Monday. Typical questions include: May teachers deduct expenses for a home office from taxes? How much is a Le Coultre, ten-karat gold wristwatch with alarm worth to collectors? How can one find out more about the Vanguard Fund? Is there a publication that evaluates annuities for a person selecting one?

Occasionally, the paper reviews a prominent business book. The "Insider" column provides behind-the-scenes glimpses of business—for example, *Forbes* magazine making a columnist of Caspar W. Weinberger, the ex-Defense Secretary. The "Techtalk" column gives readers a quick read on developments in high technology.

Dan Dorfman, the veteran financial reporter who handled *The Wall Street Journal's* "Abreast of the Market" column for years, now writes an investing column for *USA Today*. Dorfman, who sometimes seems to be working twenty-four hours a day, will step on anybody's toes to obtain a story. This is especially true if the topic concerns investing inside information.

Each column is likely to contain names of specific stocks which some of Dorfman's sources recommend. Dorfman writes as if talking with readers at a bull session over cups of coffee just after returning from a convention of America's biggest money managers.

FINANCE AND THE GENERAL PRESS

You need not subscribe to a financial publication to follow the markets. Currently, this country supports 1,645 daily newspapers, some not too well, others in grand style. Three-fourths of them belong to publishing chains and owners who can afford first-class financial coverage. Thus, even small newspapers may publish newsy business columns. It matters not to readers that the information may be syndicated around the country.

You can find financial stories in major general newspapers almost any day of the week, whether you read the *Cleveland Plain Dealer*, the *Tacoma News Tribune* or the *Milwaukee Journal*. Many more pages in the *San Francisco Chronicle* cover general rather than business news. Still, it usually publishes at least seven pages in its daily *Business* section, filling out what may be a twenty-four-page separate insert with classified adds.

Can an investor obtain enough information from such a section to forego subscribing to some of the many business and financial publications now available? Certainly, the average small investor can. If you live in the service area of the *New York Times*, the *Washington Post*, the *Boston Globe*, the *Los Angeles Times* or the *Chicago Tribune*, the volume of business and financial news in those papers may be enough to comprise a publication by itself.

The New York Times

This paper ranks its financial news highly enough to have recently changed its format to devote an entire *Business Day* section to business and investment coverage. (Previously, business and sports stories appeared combined in a second section; sports and "Living Arts" now appear in a separate section in the new three-section format.) On page one of this section, the two-column "Business Digest" summarizes the latest economic and business news. Atop the column are statistics of the Dow Jones Index, the value of the dollar against the yen, the Comex spot price of gold and the rate on thirty-year Treasury bonds.

In-depth stories cover latest developments in corporate takeover battles, interpretations of Federal Government statistical reports, personality sketches of executives who make news and other stories bearing on markets. If a business story possesses an international flavor it may be bylined by Clyde H. Farnsworth, for decades one of the best business reporters around.

Ten pages of statistics list the latest stock prices on the New York Stock Exchange, the American Exchange, the NASDAQ market and the over-the-counter market. Stock option and index option prices fill six columns. Bond prices total another three-and-a-half columns. Mutual fund quotes occupy a page, as do statistics from commodities markets.

Jan M. Rosen offers help with personal finance problems in her "Your Money" column. Stephen Labaton examines court cases of interest to investors in his "Business and the Law" column. "Media Business" is thoroughly dissected in the sub-section of that name. It receives seven columns of news space on each Monday and three columns Tuesday through Friday.

"The media is becoming as important as the people they cover," says Martin Arnold, editor of the sub-section.

Indeed, in the 1980s, the media, especially publishing, newspapers and television, offered rich returns to investors. Dun & Bradstreet's stock soared from $8.60 in 1980 to $58 in mid-1989. CBS's stock quadrupled in that time. Capital Cities/ABC's stock showed a ninefold gain. Shares of the Washington Post Company zoomed by over thirteen times in the decade.

Specific stocks in this area slipped recently. Still, smart investors watch the industry closely not only to ascertain the news, but also to recognize media companies which might experience more healthy growth over the next decade.

Arnold is a 28-year veteran of the *Times* but had no previous business reporting experience when named Media Editor. That emphasizes something stated earlier: good reporters seldom have problems developing business specialties, but few business specialists become reporters or editors.

Like *The Wall Street Journal*, the *New York Times* is a journalists' newspaper. Its key executives emerged from the reporting ranks.

The Los Angeles Times

The *Los Angeles Times* also offers a separate business section which takes itself seriously. That was evident when the paper aptly analyzed the meaning of a partnership deal negotiated by Saudi Arabia and Texaco in late December, 1988.

The story declared that the transaction "drives a wedge between the oil rich nations of the Organization of Petroleum Exporting Countries such as Saudi Arabia and the less fortunate producers of OPEC." Moreover, the pact indicated continued surpluses of petroleum on the world scene, the paper said. That story signaled caution for would-be or current oil industry investors.

The Washington Post

The same day, the *Washington Post* financial section reported the implications of Drexel Burnham Lambert's troubles concerning insider trading. The story, by David A. Vise, provided a quick, capsule explanation of junk bonds and why they have been so alluring to investors.

Local Coverage

Major money-media performers do wield influence throughout the country. Randy Shilts, a columnist with the *San Francisco Chronicle*, says: "If the television networks, national news magazines, wire services or key papers such as the *New York Times* and the *Washington Post* do not cover an issue, it does not exist in practical terms."

That irritates editors in the hinterlands, but local newspapers have some advantages. They often cover regional business developments better than do much bigger publications. Nearby companies might be too small to rate national attention. Hometown reporters and editors develop close relations (sometimes too close) with executives of the corporations. Thus, you may read more extensive stories about northern Ohio companies in the *Cleveland Plain Dealer* than you might in a national publication.

The *Boston Globe*, generally, covers the many electronic companies in suburban Boston better than outsiders do. The *Houston Post* follows Texan oil developments closer than do most out-of-state publications.

Still, no matter how well a local newspaper covers its area, news remains a hot commodity. You may obtain much from local papers. Nevertheless, you won't be assured of scoops on all local news.

For example, the *San Francisco Chronicle* provides blanket coverage of happenings in Silicon Valley below San Francisco where dozens of computer companies cluster. All often produce news as well as computers, semi-conductors, megabyte disk drives, controller boards, memory upgrades, monitors and such.

In November, 1988, a story on the front page of the *Chronicle's* business section flashed a sell warning to investors in the computer industry. The headline read: CHIP FIRMS TELL MORE BAD NEWS. Advanced Micro Devices, an area electronics company, reported layoffs of up to 1,000 employees. National Semiconductor Corp., said it expected a "significant" quarterly profit loss. Then came a litany of other dire news from companies.

Electronic companies' stocks showed declines in that same issue. That indicated many investors had heard the bad news before the *Chronicle* report. Professional investors obtain wire services flashes that usually beat the press. Dow Jones wire service, for instance, will likely summarize a major story the day before papers carry it.

SUMMARY

A newspaper balances the time factor inequities of print versus electronic journalism by printing more detailed accounts of developments. Sometimes it scoops the world. Usually it publishes an in-depth story following a television, radio or wire service news flash. Newspapers aim at providing enough information to answer the questions of most readers, including those from investors searching for new profit avenues.

If investors want more specialized information, they subscribe to financial, business and trade magazines. You, too, may find blueprints for expanding your wealth among the publications of this section of the money media.

Chapter 5

Culling Money Ideas From Magazines

A cartoon in the *London Observer* shows two characters in front of a theatre. One of them seems unenthused about the playbill. A caption reads: "I go to the theatre to be entertained. I don't want to see plays about rape, sodomy and drug addiction. I can get all that at home."

When you look for a useful publication, you scan offerings with a specific goal in mind, too. You want profitable information for your investments, information which you don't receive at home.

A MULTITUDE OF MAGAZINES

Even the average-sized newsstand is likely to offer a vast array of financial and business periodicals for your appraisal. One count showed forty-three now on sale, and this count does not include corporate publications, financial trade association magazines and the "giveaways" produced by financial promoters selling anything from gold bricks to coins, or from partnerships to precious stones.

A cursory review: *Business Week*, which describes itself in its title; *Changing Times*, a monthly providing investing and money management advice to individuals; and *Financial World*, a biweekly which profiles publicly traded companies.

Look further and you find *Fortune*, a glossy monthly which has become something more than an unread magazine in doctors' offices. *Futures* magazine, a monthly, amplifies futures and options trading. *Money* magazine shines in its bright colors, ready to tell you how to invest your money and also to spend it. *Personal Finance* depends more on subscriptions than newsstand sales, but covers the same field. *OTC Review*, an over-the-counter market publication, often focuses on fabulous growth companies.

Such magazines provide information that sharpens your investing talents. They answer questions which might stump your broker. They can show you how to make money.

Many investors cannot find time for the *Value Line Survey*, *Moody's* manuals or other services which inform only through diligent study. A financial and business magazine like *Forbes* may save you days of hard work with investing decisions.

WHAT MAGAZINES CAN DO

Magazines certainly can warn you about investing scams. They contribute insights into prospective investments. They can help you cull potential stock winners from perennial losers.

Remember, though, that magazines sometimes have long deadlines. Situations may change in that time between a story's composition and its appearance in print. A recommendation at $10 for a stock may be worthless if the share now sells for $15. So don't depend too much on magazines if you speculate or trade, rather than invest. The best recommendations cite a trading range, which offers some protection against adverse market movements.

Advice may recommend a certain stock "at $10-$11.50," or perhaps "under $11.75." If the price exceeds the advised price by the time you catch up with it, skip it. Watch the stock, though, for price dips later.

Experts advise you to buy companies with "good management" for your portfolio. Yet you have no access to executives, no easy way of evaluating them. Still, evidence of good (or bad) management lies all around.

A company's record in its annual report, 10Qs and 10K tells you something. More information comes from the long-term market record of the stock. Articles in publications provide insights into management corridors, too. Over time, you learn which periodicals provide honest information and which present sycophantic portraits of company executives.

Business Week, Forbes, Financial World and *Fortune* all analyze the merits and faults of specific corporate managers. Stories usually stress more of the first rather than of the second attributes. Nevertheless, weak praise can warn you to delve deeper into a specific company before buying its shares.

THE LATE MR. FORBES AND HIS MAGAZINE

Forbes' recently departed owner and editor-in-chief, Malcolm S. Forbes, included himself in his 400 richest Americans list and enjoyed the perks of that "club," too. He relaxed by zooming around the countryside on his Harley-Davidson motorcycle—not the usual activity for multimillionaires.

China, the Soviet Union, Pakistan, Japan, Thailand, Egypt and Turkey all hosted "friendship tours" by Forbes-led American cavalcades. They roared into town after town, spreading goodwill. Local citizens would gather in a circus atmosphere, amid exhaust fumes and noise. "We go by motorcycle from city to city in a group. Then we do a balloon trip," Forbes explained. He held six official records in this sport, and was the first to cross America in a hot air balloon.

How does all this relate to publishing business and financial news? Not much directly, but, don't be misled; a person who enjoys life to the fullest usually has a mind wide open to new ideas. That was Forbes, the man. His ideas produced one of the sharpest financial magazines in American publishing, and today *Forbes* 740,000 circulation shows it.

Forbes did the job so well that his wealth kept mounting, a fitting situation for the top man of a financial publication. His wealth proved he knew his business. Harry Schultz, the financially successful owner and editor of an international investing publication, says:

"It's a source of amazement to me that investors sometimes move hard-earned assets around on the recommendations of people who are barely making ends meet." Thus, Rule Number One for your personal investing code should be: "Give to the poor, but take your financial advice from the rich."

Forbes never publicly revealed his net worth. When wealth reaches a certain point, it becomes difficult to assess. The late J. Paul Getty, a Croesus who could distribute advice easier than he could a few dollars from his billions, liked to say: "If you can count your money, you don't have a billion dollars."

In the *Forbes* 1988 list of the super rich, Sam Moore Walton of Wal-Mart Stores topped everybody with a reputed net worth of $6.7 billion. Forbes included himself under the heading for those worth "$250 million or more." Such a broad category offers much room for error on the up side. Forbes's group comrades included Marshall Field V, Gordon Peter Getty, Estee Lauder, Ralph Lauren, William J. Paley, Meshulam Riklis, William Wrigley and a few others who aren't short of cash.

The *New York Daily News* termed Forbes "a billionaire." *Newsday* estimated his wealth at $400 million to $700 million. Forbes admitted only to owning his magazine plus "a few other things." Those "things" included a Colorado ranch measured in square miles, a South Sea island, a Tangier palace, a French chateau, a London mansion, a dozen Russian Czarist jeweled eggs (two more than the Kremlin!) plus rare collections of art, presidential letters and toy soldiers. He flew in his own Boeing 727, christened "Capitalist Tool," and he voyaged in his own 151-foot yacht.

When a person achieves such wealth, his or her exact worth really doesn't matter. As John Jacob Astor, the 19th century tycoon, said: "A man who has a million dollars is as well off as if he were rich."

Forbes, *the Magazine*

Forbes, a full-color publication, certainly attracts attention on a newsstand, with its title lettered in green, red, yellow or gold. From three to six provocative headlines share space with the cover picture. Some issues have run to 430 pages.

"31 Turnarounds—Good Bets to Outperform the Market," reads one headline. "Why Are Economists' Forecasts So Bad?," asks another. "What the Big Money Managers Are Buying," is a third. A special annual issue prints the *Forbes* title in gold, with one headline occupying the entire cover: "The Richest People in America." Inside, the magazine names 400 of these elite individuals, cites their estimated net worth and summarizes how they accumulated their wealth. Study their stories to pick up any relevant money-making ideas that might help your portfolio.

Credit Forbes for selecting the right people to produce his publication. Editor James W. Michaels ably filled that role since 1961. Of him, Forbes said: "My own life-style, the balloons and such, create an awareness of the magazine. But, Jim gave it a whole fresh look. He is probably the single most significant influence on business journalism in our time."

Michaels describes the magazine in a nutshell: "Have confidence in Adam Smith. Trust the free markets to bust monopolies, nourish entrepreneurship and create jobs. That's the philosophy behind every page of *Forbes* magazine." He adds: "We try to develop insights into what is happening."

In recent years, he did that with much help from now-retired Managing Editor Sheldon Zalaznick, who welcomed ideas from members of the staff at all levels, from the plebeians to the hierarchy.

The Layout of Forbes *Magazine*

The publication is divided into sections: Companies, Industries, Economics, Government, Personalities, International, Investing, On the Docket (law), Numbers Game (accounting or statistics), Marketing, Science and Technology, Computers/Communications, Careers, Faces Behind the Figures, Columnists, Money & Investments (tables and indexes) and Departments. The last section embraces ten features such as "Readers Say," "Follow Through" (updates of earlier stories), "Commentary" and so on.

The Magazine's Coverage

Cover story topics range from a profile of Banker James Wolfensohn to one concerning the computer-communications information overload, and from the gaming industries of Las Vegas and Atlantic City to an interview with Nobel Laureate Milton Friedman.
Investing stories offer ideas for readers. One explains where Richard Rainwater, a secretive Texan money wizard, invests his money. Another warns how mutual fund mergers transform a non-performing fund into one without *any* record to scare potential new investors. Over time, *Forbes* cites dozens of investing opportunities or pitfalls. Stories of successful or troubled companies provide more investing insights into specific situations.
The magazine likes humor. One issue quoted the late Soviet leader Nikita Khrushchev: "Politicians are the same all over. They promise to build a bridge even where there is no river." Another *Forbes* item, written by Jerry Smith, quoted *Motorcyclist Magazine*. It read:

> Question: *A lot of people who are opposed to helmet laws (for motorcyclists) claim helmets can cause accidents. Is this true?*
> Answer: *A helmet can cause an accident if you run over one on the freeway and fall down.*
> Question: *What if I'm still not convinced helmets work?*
> Answer: *Try this experiment. Put on a helmet and have a friend whack you on the head with a baseball bat. Now, try the same experiment without the helmet. If you still are not convinced, you probably are too hard-headed to need a helmet.*

One short squib quotes the *Benton County [Mo.] Enterprise*. It read: "A newspaper carried the following classified: 'For sale, complete set of encyclopedias, an atlas, almanacs. Never used. Teenage son knows everything."
Even if you read the magazine regularly, you will not learn everything about investing. But you *will* have many more profitable ideas than when you started.

BUSINESS WEEK IS SERIOUS BUSINESS

Business Week, Fortune and *Financial World* are *Forbes'* competitors, each with its own distinctive format and way of presenting information. The weekly *Business Week* long has been McGraw-Hill's premiere publication among several in its stable.

McGraw-Hill, with $2 billion annual sales, caters to business management as well as textbook and engineering markets. It possesses niches in specialized fields with such publications as *Aviation Week, Chemical Week* and *Engineering News-Record,* in addition to *Business Week.*

Late in 1988 the company restructured operations, but *Business Week* remains the bright light of its empire. Over the years it has made the transition from a narrowly segmented weekly to one with nearly a million-reader circulation.

Inside Business Week

The magazine takes itself seriously and wants readers to do the same. It presents stories objectively; it reports the news without personal opinions. There is little room for the philosophy or humor found in sections of *Forbes.* You will find opinions only on the editorial page. Protectionism mounts in foreign trade, warns one such piece, and goes on to say that this is an illusory remedy for balancing trade deficits.

Each issue contains a cover story on a major trend. A dozen or more news stories appear in its *Top of the News* section. More stories fall into compartmentalized segments, such as Economic Analysis, International, Government, Science & Technology, People, The Corporation, Marketing, Finance, Information Processing, Social Issues and Personal Business.

The magazine offers investing advice, but not as an oracle. A prominent money manager is likely to state the main theme in quotes. The magazine lets readers form their own opinions from these statements. Obviously, quote selection requires some subjectivity by editors. But, with this system, it can claim to being a news rather then an advisory or opinion publication.

A Scandal

Business Week's "Inside Wall Street" page does provide investing tips which market professionals take seriously—sometimes too seriously. That was evident in 1988 when curious market upswings developed in stocks named on that page.

Prices of quoted stocks climbed just before stories appeared in the magazine. This suggested that insiders leaked contents to market players ahead of publication dates.

An investigation traced the problem to independent printers. They were divulging data to sources in that period between receipt of copy for printing and release of finished magazines.

The scandal tarnished *Business Week*, though no one from the publication was directly involved. Not so with another case. One staff radio broadcaster invested small sums for his own account in companies mentioned favorably on his program. The announcer lost his job, leaving the magazine's editors red-faced.

Stock Tips

The "Inside Wall Street" column does indeed carry weight. In March, 1989, it reported that Boeing Co. was exploring takeover of rival Lockheed Corp. The day the story appeared, shares of both companies jumped by nearly two points each.

The magazine finds interesting situations useful for portfolio building. One story noted how junk mail proliferates in mail boxes around the country, even as companies spend less money for advertising in newspapers and on television. Advo-System, the nation's largest direct mail company, benefits, the story said. The stock sold for $6 a share at the time. In a quote, a money manager claimed the price could soar to $30 a share by 1990. It reached a less towering $11.87 in May, 1990.

Another story featured a turnaround situation. Stock of Summit Health Ltd., a hospital-nursing home operator, collapsed from $5.50 in early 1987 to $1.50 in February, 1988. "But Summit may be about to regain its strength," the periodical said. It did, but not by much. Summit stock stood at $1.75 a share in May, 1990.

Periodically, the magazine looks at mutual funds, names the star performers over the past year and last three years. The data helps identify buys for fund investors.

MONEY LIVES UP TO ITS TITLE

Time, Inc., offers two magazines in the financial and business field, both with general appeal. *Money*, a monthly, aims at the personal and family finance field; *Fortune*, a bi-weekly, covers business management. Both are glossy, full-color magazines produced with the sophistication one might expect from a publishing giant like Time.

A random check of *Money* cover stories indicates its focus: "5 SMART FINANCIAL MOVES TO MAKE NOW"; "100 BEST INVESTMENTS FOR THE 1990'S"; "WHAT EVERY FAMILY NEEDS TO KNOW ABOUT MONEY"; "HOW TO CUT YOUR TAXES BY APRIL."

Money's *Contents*

The magazine offers career guidance to readers. It explains how to utilize financial planning, suggests investing strategies and offers stock picks. It warns about financial pitfalls. It clarifies insurance needs and available policies. It focuses upon retirement nest-egg building and the problems of adjusting to retirement rocking chairs. It tells readers how to finance college educations for the kids.

Sometimes the magazine tries too hard to be all things to all people. Stories for newlyweds appear beside those for senior citizens. Every issue is likely to offer stories of no relevance to you, yet every issue probably contains something of interest to you as well.

A Human Touch

Money features more human interest stories than you find in most financial or business publications. Each issue includes one or more features about a couple's finances. *The Wall Street Journal* pioneered such stories a few decades ago. *Money* refined the technique and added a few touches of its own.

After detailing a couple's position, financial planners suggest solutions for problems. Net worth statistics allow readers to observe the personal affairs of story subjects for comparisons with their own situations.

Stories sometimes read like soap opera scripts. In one issue appears the financial tale of Tim and Jane George, Honolulu teachers who made a career move to Japan. Another describes the investing problems of Dick and Mona Divine, a Yellowstone Park Ranger couple wintering amid Wyoming's snows. A third story examines the problems of Marc and Melanine Walker of Ithaca, New York, a dual-income family raising two young boys.

Money also provides investing ideas, like the 100 best investments for the 1990's mentioned earlier. That *Money* list ranges from Aluminum Co. of America stock to zero coupon U.S. Treasury bonds, from American Express shares to those of Waste Management.

CHANGING TIMES'S INDIVIDUAL STYLE

This monthly competes with *Money* for readers. It, too, covers personal finance, insurance, investing, taxes, retirement planning, estate building, home mortgages and such without too much technical data. Yet it offers its own service-oriented slant. It suggests ways to save money through wise spending as well as citing avenues for low-risk investing.

For years the magazine printed an optimistic quote from Ralph Waldo Emerson, the essayist, on its title page. It read: "This time, like all times, is a very good one if we but know what to do with it." The upbeat line summarized the publication's philosophy.

A New Philosophy

The January, 1989, issue shelved that quote. In its place came one written by the magazine's founder, W.M. Kiplinger, for the first issue in 1946. It reads: "The times will always be changing. Much of life and work consists of looking for changes in advance and figuring out what to do about them. This publication will try to help you peer ahead and see straight." This now is the magazine's philosophy.

Changing Times' *Contents*

The five-section cover story of that January, 1989, issue presented an optimistic picture of the 1990s: for the economy, for investing, for home prices, for inflation and for leisure time.

Optimism in strong doses may seem bland. It reminds us too much of Voltaire's Pangloss, who blithely met all trouble by saying: "All is for the best, in this best of possible worlds."

A Coin Selling Expose

But *Changing Times* is far from being a pollyanna publication. Frequently, it prints tough, investigative pieces with information you won't find easily elsewhere. In February, 1989, for instance, the magazine scored coin collecting frauds. The headline baldly declared: "HEADS YOU LOSE, TAILS YOU LOSE."

The article described how high-pressure telephone salespeople offer nonexistent coin bargains. They promise buy-backs should you have second thoughts about deals. Then they disappear with your money, leaving you with hard-to-sell coins worth less than half the purchase price.

Sellers suffer, too. Scam artists may offer to sell any coins you have at high prices in nonexistent auctions for a small fee. Once they obtain your collection, they vanish.

Rare coins may sell at high prices if in mint condition. Unfortunately, most coins on the market don't fit that classification. Their prices increase only slightly, if at all, over time. Still, you hear claims that coins beat inflation better than any other investment.

Changing Times explained how this myth developed. Salomon, Inc., a reputable brokerage house, periodically estimates returns supposedly achieved by coin collectors. Its figures show a 15.1 percent average return annually over the last twenty years.

The data sounds wonderful until you realize it means virtually nothing to you. Salomon bases its estimates on the value of a *hypo-*

thetical, not real, coin portfolio. "The figures do not represent actual sales and are not adjusted for insurance, storage or transaction costs," said _Changing Times_. Scam artists do not tell you this.

Coin World, a trade publication, compiles a better price index. It uses actual prices of transactions through each year and covers 16,576 grades of coins. Through 1983-1988, the index averaged a 2.5 percent annual gain, far below the 8 percent plus offered by safe, very liquid money funds in recent times.

If you like collecting coins as a hobby, deal only with reputable merchandisers. Such dealers, through the Industry Council for Tangible Assets, have developed a dealer certification program aimed at driving out shysters. For a free directory of the nearly eighty companies which passed muster for the accreditation, write to Coin and Bullion Dealer Accreditation Program, 25 E St. NW, Eighth Floor, Washington, DC 20001.

If you read that _Changing Times_ story you might conclude that coin collecting makes a fine hobby but a poor investment. If you still want more information about coins, look up such trade magazines as _Coin World, Coins, The Coin Enthusiast's Journal_ and _World Coin News_ (addresses are provided in the appendix).

FORTUNE'S APPEAL

Fortune built its reputation by focusing on managers of businesses rather than investors _per se_ in its articles. The magazine does offer a _Personal Investing_ section, but tailors it for the executive with dollars to spare, not for small-time investors.

The bulk of the magazine's stories concern corporations, their executives and the reasons for company results. Typical story headlines include: "GM'S TASK AHEAD"; "HOW TO GET CUSTOMERS TO LOVE YOU"; "BUSINESS HALL OF FAME"; "YES, YOU CAN MANAGE FOR THE LONG TERM," and "SEVEN KEYS TO BUSINESS LEADERSHIP."

Marshall Loeb, _Fortune's_ managing editor, is a veteran of Time's publication empire who could write a sparkling financial piece himself. Its editorial board includes the likes of Edmund Faltermayer, Gene Bylinsky and Louis Kraar, each with decades of experience, and bright women like Carol Junge Loomis, Julie Connelly and Susan Fraker. They produce a sophisticated publication which no longer can be termed "bland"—a charge heard a few years ago.

FINANCIAL WORLD EXPANDS COVERAGE

This biweekly magazine with a circulation of 440,000 covers management, too. "UNDER TOUGH BILL ESREY [chief executive] UNITED TELECOM HAS NEW RESPECT," reads one title. An upbeat piece analyzes how Scott McNealy, chief executive of Sun Microsystems, leads his firm deeper into computer work stations. "For now, investors (in it) can quit worrying," the magazine concludes.

Another story spotlights Warner-Lambert's chairman. "By making Warner-Lambert nearly as profitable as Merck, Joe Williams runs the risk of raiders taking a bite out of his company," it says.

Star Stocks Picked

The magazine analyzed the research of a dozen major drug companies during the 1980s. It ranked Glaxo Holdings at the top, Merck & Co., second, Pfizer third and Upjohn fourth. Another story named the twenty-five companies with the best ten-year stock price records. Wal-Mart Stores headed the list, with a 6,580 percent gain in its stock. Cray Research ranked second, with 5,006 percent.

The list continues with Toys 'R' us, third at 3,418 percent; The Gap, fourth at 2,764 percent; and Safety-Kleen, fifth at 2,006 percent. The next five in order are: Computer Associates; Tyco Laboratories; Glaxo Holdings (ADR); Marriott; and Honda Motors (ADR).

Financial World often expresses familiarity with its subjects, i.e., "Bill" rather than "William," "Joe" rather than "Joseph." Sometimes, of course, a publication grows too familiar with sources. Stories may become publicity puffs as editors flatter their friends. However, *Financial World* reports managerial goofs as well as successes. Not long ago, it published its list of "the worst managers" currently in American industry. It, also, looked unfavorably at SmithKline Beckman and its chairman, Henry Wendt. "The rise and fall of SmithKline is a sad tale of lost opportunity and management incompetence," said the magazine.

The Staff

Dan Cordtz, a feisty newsperson, serves as Chief Correspondent. He spent years with *The Wall Street Journal* and *Fortune*, then did duty as Economics Editor for the American Broadcasting Co. An imposing list of columnists reports various aspects of finance and business. Stephen Taub, Senior Editor and "Market Watch" columnist, pulls no punches with companies. Recapitalization does not always pay off, he wrote, after analyzing USG Corp., the parent of U.S. Gypsum. "My advice is to get out quick," he said.

THE OTC REVIEW FOCUSES ON SMALL STOCKS

This monthly covers a lively investing area. Editor Robert Flaherty says: "We cover the fastest growing securities market in the world. We study the management of companies traded over-the-counter and act as critics reviewing their performances. We aspire to be 'the shareholder's friend.'"

The OTC market includes growing companies with rising prospect. Early buyers profit from their stocks, but they may lose heavily if the companies stumble. *OTC Review* helps keep readers on track.

THE ERUDITE *ECONOMIST:* THE BRITISH VIEW

A different perspective comes from *The Economist*, a London-based weekly which also sells in America. In erudite style, it blankets international and political affairs, presents world business and financial sections and offers a condensed U.S. news segment. You may learn something extra from the magazine, too. For instance, did you know that Benjamin Franklin developed bifocal glasses in 1784 to help his own eyes, and that Aids, in transmission, resembles Hepatitis B?

The Economist *Explains And Entertains*

A story on bankruptcy explained that "bankrupt" comes from the Latin, meaning "broken bench." Tradesmen labored on their workbenches, and borrowed from lenders to finance operations. If a worker failed to pay debts, creditors physically smashed his bench, leaving him an unemployed pauper.

A story about Italian banking cites Monte dei Paschi di Siena as the world's oldest bank. Founded by Franciscan friars in 1472, it operated continuously ever since. Today, it is Italy's most profitable bank.

The *Science & Technology* section notes breakthroughs in high-tech, medicine, gene splicing and other areas. One story cites gallium arsenide as the new wonder material in electronics.

GENERAL NEWS MAGAZINES

Time and *Newsweek* occasionally print deeply reported economic features, but not often enough to rate as financial magazines. *U.S. News & World Report*, a junior general news competitor, regularly presents a useful business page.

When other publications warned that the Japanese "are buying up America," *U.S. News & World Report* calmly reviewed the situation. True, it stated, foreigners own 10 percent of U.S. manufacturing, 20 percent of U.S. banking and 46 percent of downtown Los Angeles. But look at that in a broad context, advised the magazine. In 1988, the United States held $309 billion in overseas assets—18 percent more than foreigners had in this country. Moreover, Britain, not Japan, topped foreign investors here with a $75 billion stake, said the magazine. Japan's $33.4 billion ran third, behind the $47 billion of the Netherlands.

REGIONAL BUSINESS MAGAZINES

Publications like *Crain's Detroit Business* or *California Business* generally, focus on management not investing. You may learn more about area companies than you care to, but that could prove useful if you concentrate investments in a specific region.

FINANCIAL PROFESSIONAL JOURNALS

If you enjoy broadening your investing knowledge, study the journals of the investing fraternity. You won't find such publications on too many newsstands, except perhaps in New York's lower Manhattan. You might see them on your broker's desk or encounter them in a good business library. Once in a while their promotional literature finds its way into your mailbox.

Such publications include the *Wall Street Transcript*, the *Journal of Finance*, *The Journal of Portfolio Management*, *Institutional Investor*, the *Financial Analysts Journal*, the *Investment Dealers Digest* and a few dozen more.

Some intellectuals and business executives like the management stories of *Harvard Business Review* and other "Ivory Tower" publications. Market technicians like the monthly *Technical Analysis of Stocks & Commodities* (circulation 15,000). Here you read stories on new computer software and utilities for investors and how-to articles about technical analysis. Charts and graphs illustrate everything. A little humor is offered in the form of cartoons and in reports of unusual market incidents.

Brokers read *Securities Week* and the *Bond Buyer*, as well as the *Stockbroker*. These focus upon aspects of jobs and business in brokers' offices. *The Stockmarket* looks at behind-the-scenes activities when you purchase shares. Security analysts may prefer *Institutional Investor*, which annually names the brightest analysts in the business, or the *Survey of Wall Street Research* or the *Financial Analysts Journal*.

The Wall Street Transcript

This thick tabloid brings readers every company analytical report that emerges from brokerage houses, plus much more. Unfortunately, the average investor can't afford its expensive subscription rate of $1,680 a year. The *Transcript* really shines when it publishes the taped recordings of a security analysts' gathering. Often, such meetings focus upon a particular industry, i.e., appliances, computers, utilities, agricultural implements, retailing or any of dozens others. You can learn more about the investing side of an industry from these printed discussions than you could at the actual meetings, for you can study the comments at leisure.

That ability to study investment strategies and recommendations in a relaxed atmosphere may be one reason why television financial programs catch the attention of millions of current and potential investors. Is the televised money media merely entertainment? Or is it a serious money enterprise whereby you can collect profitable ideas? For an answer to those questions, let's look at financial television.

Chapter 6

Money Tips On The Air Waves

Before we meet tonight's special guest, let's take a look at . . . ."
The rest of that line differs every week, but if you catch that
phrase when switching stations on your television set you'll recognize the speaker. Louis Rukeyser, the silver-haired, witty star of
Public Service Broadcasting's (PBS) "Wall Street Week," no longer
needs an introduction to his five million viewers. For twenty years,
he has dominated the world of television investment advice, the
electronic-era financial advisor who keeps you interested in money
throughout his half-hour show.

Rukeyser virtually created the television personal finance program. When he launched his show in 1970, major TV networks
viewed a financial feature as something about as interesting to dra-
matize as an accountants' convention. It took PBS to change that
opinion, at least with TV viewers.

Even today, the big three networks possess little faith in the
drawing power of such shows. ABC's "Business World" remains
the only major network money production on the air. Networks
shoehorn financial stories into general news programs, or don't
bother with them at all. You might catch the Dow Jones Industrial
Index at market close, but not much else.

Cable and PBS lead in TV financial coverage. Radio has created
its own lively niche. Neither threatens print publishing, but they do
siphon advertising dollars from the money media pool.

ENTERTAINMENT? OR SERIOUS ADVICE?

One certainly can question the value of television as an information source for investors. Rukeyser's program ranks as one of the best of the breed. But is it a relaxer, or a visual supplement to *The Wall Street Journal?* Can someone obtain worthwhile tips from such programs for transformation into cash?

The answers, of course, lie within the minds of viewers, not those of program producers. Smart investors translate nearly every experience into something useful for portfolios. Others, perhaps the majority, absorb only the entertainment.

Unless such programs offer showmanship, they do not succeed. Anyone who watches Rukeyser, Jerry Goodman of the popular "Adam Smith's Money World," or Paul Kangas of PBS's "The Nightly Business Report," realizes that they all possess the flair of snake-oil salesmen of a bygone era. Yesterday's patent medicine peddlers are today's hosts, emoting before TV cameras, with less melodrama and much more knowledge of their subjects.

Certainly if you regard finance as an awesome topic with a lexicon akin to the vocabulary of Sikkim, then a TV money show provides a different perspective for viewing the subject. It concentrates on easily understandable market fundamentals. Talk, sprinkled with quips, succeeds better than charts with jagged lines. To viewers, endorsement of a company's stock means more than the share's thirty-nine-day advance-decline pattern.

"WALL STREET WEEK"

Rukeyser's show avoids the technical jargon which can be deadly dull to all but the confirmed financial elf. Rukeyser coined the term "elf" to denote the technical analyst who uses statistics to time the market's swings. When he employs the reference (usually in the plural) he is likely to smile sardonically, as if sharing his secret distrust of technicians with his audience.

Sometimes, though, Rukeyser's attitude is not so subtle. When Robert R. Prechter, an eminent technical analyst, appeared on the show in February, 1988, he faced a barrage of critical comment which verged on ridicule from his host. Prechter publishes the *El-*

liott Wave Theorist and is the chief apostle of this method of market interpretation (see Chapter 9). He contends markets move in waves which may be deciphered through statistical analysis.

The idea sounds like something brewed by the witches from *Macbeth*. Yet, Wall Street generally regards Prechter as one of the best market timers in the investment advisory field. In early 1981, he predicted that gold would sink to $388 an ounce. It bottomed to within a few cents of $388 that August. He followed with a string of other accurate forecasts. But early in 1987, with the stock market soaring, he predicted something he later regretted.

He speculated that the Dow Jones Industrial Average would hit 3686 in the great bull market then underway. He reversed himself before the October 19, 1987 Crash, but not quickly enough to warn all of his letter subscribers to sell everything.

Rukeyser relayed this fact to viewers as he introduced his guest that February night. Then, as he faced an embarrassed Prechter, he asked, rhetorically: "Isn't it time you faced the facts and admitted publicly that all that old headline-grabbing talk of yours about a Grand Super Cycle taking us to 3686 was just some kind of intellectual mumbo jumbo?"

Prechter smiled weakly, like a man invited to his own birthday party only to have a jack-in-the-box jump from the first gift package opened. The Yale '71 psychology graduate and Mensa member seldom becomes ruffled. Socially, he remains the quiet intellectual, almost apologetic in manner as if fearful of attracting attention.

Red-faced, he listened as Rukeyser finished the introduction with a question concerning the letter writer's sudden switch to a bearish position. ". . . will Prechter the pessimist turn out to be any more reliable than Prechter the optimist?"

"Lou, I'm shocked," Prechter responded.

Indeed he looked it as he struggled to recover his aplomb. The program continued lamely through the half hour. One suspects, however, that Prechter did not linger long in the studio later.

The Show's Impact

Rukeyser does not usually skewer his guests. However, he does needle the rotating members of his panel when comparing stock picks made earlier with subsequent results. Panelists and guests take it willingly, for careers can be made on the program.

Investment letter writers obtain publicity worth thousands of dollars in added subscriptions per appearance. Money managers enjoy upward spurts in reputations. Promoters of financial seminars bid for the services of Rukeyser's stars. Strangers greet Rukeyser panel veterans like Frank Cappiello and Carter Randall as television personalities in their own right.

Rukeyser is the father figure on the program. He is supported by a three-member panel which he assembles from approximately two dozen regulars. All take turns querying that program's guest, who might be a money manager, a brokerage official, an investment letter writer or anybody else in the money field.

No readily apparent continuity exists with these programs. One exudes optimism about the market; a week later, pessimism reigns. Emphasis favors bonds one week, stocks another and neither on the following program. Viewers must sort it out themselves.

Rukeyser understands finance and the free enterprise system. He prods guests and panelists into specific stock recommendations. He makes none himself. His basic question among his sharp queries on every show is: "What should investors do now?" Then, he lets others answer. That may be one of the secrets of his success. Making no predictions or stock selections, he can't be embarrassed by a wrong forecast. He remains above the fray; the wise interlocutor asking questions you yourself might ask of money gurus.

A Money Man Rates The Program

Do any of the show's stock tips pay off? That depends on who does the picking. After appearing on the program several times over the years, Charles Allmon, Editor, *Growth Stock Outlook*, sought to answer that question for his readers.

He first appeared as a guest in October, 1979, and again in October, 1980. He recommended twelve stocks as good buys on the first program and fourteen on the second, with four of the first twelve repeating in 1980.

Suppose someone had invested $1,000 in each of those stocks on the first trading day after hearing the recommendations, held the investments and collected all dividends? As of September 1, 1988, twenty-three of those twenty-six stocks increased in value by from 9 percent to 1,351 percent each. The $26,000 investment would have become $107,227 for an annual compounded rate of return of 18.59 percent for the first batch of shares and 18.30 percent for the second. Obviously, had dividends been reinvested, the returns would have been higher.

Says Allmon: "If anyone tells you that no one can beat the averages, our record refutes such doubters. As for "Wall Street Week," here is hard evidence that highly useful information is available for serious investors."

That record says a lot, too, about the buy-and-hold investing system which Allmon follows. Warren Buffett, Mario Gabelli, John Templeton, Peter Lynch and other super investors also may hold investments awhile in anticipation of higher payoffs, but the mere practice of holding for long periods is not enough. These investors select only the stocks which meet their investing criteria, and they emphasize this should they appear on any television financial shows. If investors watching "Wall Street Week" learn only what buy-and-hold means when practiced by the masters, they will be amply rewarded for time spent before their sets.

ADAM SMITH, THE INTELLECTUAL ADVISOR

Another buy-and-hold man does well on television, too. George Jerome Waldo Goodman, star of "Adam Smith's Money World," confesses that some of his personal holdings may lay in his portfolio for fifteen years. You won't hear him recommending anything on his PBS program, though, not even indirectly through his guests.

Most of America knows Goodman as Adam Smith, a pen name he adopted when writing for *New York Magazine*, a publication he co-founded in 1967. In 1968, he wrote *The Money Game*, using the *nom-de-plume*. It proved to be one of the funniest and most successful books to emerge from Wall Street, and it firmly established his pseudonym. Today, friends know him as Jerry and the business and intellectual world knows him as George J.W., but to his readers and TV viewers he remains Adam Smith.

An Economics Class For Viewers

Goodman explains the factors affecting markets, without selecting any specific shares for investments. The two million viewers who watch him probably absorb more of Economics 101 from his show than they ever did in college. They are also encouraged to think for themselves. On the air, Goodman fosters an erudite, Ivory Tower approach, which befits a Rhodes Scholar and chairman of the Advisory Council of Princeton University's Economics Department.

His programs focus upon a key economic topic each week—the rate of unemployment, the strength of the dollar, the inflation trend or whatever catches his fancy. He analyzes each subject in-depth, and smoothly interviews authorities who illustrate the issues. He terms the show's approach "a portfolio manager's outlook." A money manager—which Goodman was for a couple of years on Wall Street—watches economic events closely and estimates how developments will affect the holdings under his or her management, then reacts to enhance or protect them. In his programs, Goodman translates this process into information which may help viewers manage their own portfolios.

PUBLIC SERVICE BROADCASTING (PBS)

Rukeyser and Goodman (Smith) provide the financial feature interest on PBS. "The Nightly Business Report" presents the day's money news in straightforward style to an estimated two million viewers.

Paul Kangas, an ex-stockbroker who has become an affable television host, understands the market and what investors want to know. He takes viewers directly into the key business stories of the day and he explains facts without injecting opinions. His wrap-ups of stock market action make viewers aware of what happened. Commentaries by Martin Feldstein, former chairman of the presidential Council of Economic Advisors, provide an insider's perspective on market-affecting economic developments.

DOW JONES ON THE AIR

Dow Jones, parent of *The Wall Street Journal*, carves a spot for itself in television backed by its vast business and financial news empire. It markets brief nightly news segments to any interested stations for inclusion in their news roundups. Its half-hour show, ably anchored by Consuelo Mack, appears weekly on 100 stations. A daily, live broadcast to TV-Tokyo is translated there into Japanese.

MAJOR NETWORKS COMPETE WEAKLY

Big network television has no Rukeyser, Adam Smith, Kangas nor Consuelo Mack. They do have good financial reporters like Ray Brady and Robert Krulwich at CBS, Mike Jensen at NBC and a few others. They are the "minutemen" of television. Their bosses squeeze them into short, breathless presentations of topics, each of which probably filled two columns in *The Wall Street Journal* that day.

The "Big Three" television networks provide no time for economic explanations. Even when a major money development explodes into general news, misconceptions sometimes warp the script.

"If Thomas Edison were to invent the light bulb today, the CBS Evening News would lead off with Dan Rather somberly announcing that disaster has just struck the candlestick industry," says Robert M. Bleiberg, editorial page editor of *Barron's* and a long-time critic of television's handling of business news.

Media Institute Criticizes Networks

Bleiberg's views gained support in 1988 from a study by the Media Institute, a non-profit news research foundation. Ted Smith III, an associate professor at the School of Mass Communications at Virginia Commonwealth University, headed the research. Using Vanderbilt Television News Archives at Vanderbilt University, he analyzed 14,000 economic broadcasts through 1982-87 at ABC, CBS and NBC.

His conclusion: "Coverage consistently emphasized economic problems and de-emphasized or omitted economic successes." Moreover, from the beginning of the research period to the end, networks steadily reduced their coverage of the key economic indicators which mean so much to investors. In that period, the number of stories devoted to such key numbers as unemployment, inflation, personal income and utilization of capacity fell from 1,022 in the first year to 373 in the last.

"The reduction in coverage of economic indicators had become so great that it would be difficult for someone who relied on network evening news as his sole source of information to be adequately informed about economic affairs," said the author.

Criticism Mounts

Dan Cordtz, ABC's former economics editor, offers a telling insider's view of big network financial coverage. He reports that his bosses equated economic news with castor oil, something for sugar-coating. Says Cordtz: "They always wanted the same story, a chick-enshit one and a half-minute piece about some economic statistic that came out that day." His opinion concerning why financial news usually falls flat before large, network audiences: "My own feeling about it is that the average television viewer doesn't give a shit about the stock market."

His bitterness stems from experience. Cordtz departed from ABC in late 1987 to create a business news program for syndication to stations. He found almost no interest in the idea. Now, he is a senior editor at the magazine *Financial World*.

The Problem For The Networks

Perhaps television moguls should not be judged too harshly. Financial news offers few opportunities for programs that rely on visual formats. Sports broadcasting requires little more than good camera work when Joe Montana fades back to pass with a Forty-Niner game on the line. Footage of violence and conflict appears on almost any news show. But a fifty-point jump in the Dow Jones Index, which rates as news to investors, is difficult to transform into a thrilling fifteen- to thirty-second visual.

Moreover, all those millions of investors affected by market swings may watch television only for entertainment. They receive their hot financial news from a computer screen, a stock ticker, a telephone, or from their background and analysis from the financial press. They may not even tune to a business show.

Network television plays to the ratings. ABC's half-hour Sunday morning show, "Business World," outlasted all other Big Three productions to survive as the only remaining major net business show. Hosted by Sander Vanocur, a thorough television professional but not an investment advisor, the show plods along.

PBS succeeds where major networks fail because it operates at a lower cost level. Moreover, advertisers don't dictate programming and its viewers want something more than mass entertainment.

WHY CABLE SUCCEEDS

Meanwhile, business news finds a good home on cable television, which reached 78 million U.S. households at start of 1989 and is expanding at a 7 percent rate annually. Here, the nature of the business calls for programs tailored for smaller, specific audiences. Money shows fit easily into this pattern.

Ted Turner's Network

Ted Turner, chief of Cable News Network (CNN) and its companion chains, realized cable's potential before most broadcasters did. He saw it as a better platform than big, flashy networks for general news, including business and financial programs. CNN now thrives with 168 hours of news programming and 53 million subscribers. Its offshoot, "Headline News," has 35 million. Business shows cover markets in key time slots through the day.

In 1988, the *New York Times* analyzed CNN and concluded: "CNN represents the most innovative development in television news in the quarter century since CBS and NBC . . . offered the first half-hour evening news programs. And CNN is unique. The Big Three are entertainment networks, with news appendages. For CNN, news is the only business."

CNN's Programming

The network opens its financial coverage with "Business Morning" at 6:30 A.M. Eastern time for an audience of 200,000 anchored by Stuart Varney and Deborah Marchini. The show covers important developments in overseas markets. It also anticipates business developments for the day.

"Business Day" follows with a half hour show at 7:30 A.M., for its audience of a quarter of a million viewers. It updates major stories of "Business Morning," and includes personal finance features.

Key business and financial stories receive play on news programs through the day. "Moneyline," the nightly business news report, wraps up the day's events. It gives broad coverage of stock markets for an average 300,000 viewers.

Lou Dobbs, the knowledgeable anchor, hosts the show smoothly. But this is a team effort. Myron Kandel contributes interpretations of specific happenings; Dan Dorfman, the stock sleuth from *USA Today*, may offer a stock tip or two. Correspondents contribute. Everything moves with dispatch.

"Your Money," a popular CNN financial program, draws an audience of a quarter of a million on Saturday and double that on Sunday. Among other things, it offers the week's wrapup of mutual fund and certificate of deposit quotes for income investors. "Inside Business" offers interviews of corporate executives by the CNN news staff for an audience of 200,000.

FINANCIAL NEWS NETWORK

CNN recognized business coverage as a necessary part of general news and created a reporting machine to support it. Smaller cable companies, however, sometimes allowed hucksters to rent time on facilities. In the mid-1980s, this created what state prosecuting attorneys and Better Business Bureaus called "Get-Rich-Quick-Television." At least a score of these programs offered viewers a chance, allegedly, to become millionaires overnight, usually in real estate. Viewers first were required to take courses obtainable for up to $395 each by mail or at seminars.

As disillusioned people demanded money back, these shows folded. By 1988, most were gone and consolidation had started among cable companies.

Financial News Network (FNN) emerged from the chaos. Ted Turner, chief stockholder of CNN, wanted to add FNN's 32-million home system to its operations, but the directors prevented the merger.

Meanwhile, FNN gathers strength from a slow start. The cable network lost $22 million in its first four years and survived only by slashing staff by two-thirds to only forty-two employees during the dark days of 1984.

Since 1986, it has operated in the black and now employs several hundred. Weekday programming in September 1990 offered twenty-four hours of business news daily to 35 million subscribers.

In the past, advertising on FNN sometimes masqueraded as market information. What seemed to be investment advice really were sales pitches for financial planners, gold sellers and such.

In its May 8, 1989, issue, *Barron's* published a letter from a retired stockbroker who had been watching FNN with fascination. He wrote: "I have called many of the toll-free numbers of various securities, commodity and information peddlers who advertise on FNN. I have kept score on an irregular basis of investment results. They all resulted in losses."

Stung by such criticism, FNN now works to avoid questionable advertising. The you-can-get-rich theme no longer prevails. FNN's slogan is now: "FNN, You Have No Business Watching Anything Else." (In justice to the network, it should be pointed out that deceptive advertising plagues most of the money media, not just cable TV.).

FNN Builds Support

Investors like the stock market quotes which run constantly below FNN's screen and many keep their sets continuously on cable to follow those prices. They closely watch the half-hour "Business This Morning" or the "Market Wrap" shows.

FNN's tie-in with United Press International may bolster programming. Its sophisticated one-hour weekly pay program, "Investors' Advantage," represents the TV equivalent of the investment newsletter. "Investors News Release Watch" brings corporate news releases to viewers four times a day, long before newspapers publish them.

CHALLENGES TO CABLE

NBC battles FNN for the market with its 24-hour Consumer News and Business Channel (CNBC). With entry into 13 million homes, it has a way to go, needing 30 million viewers to break even. But its parent, General Electric Company, has deep pockets.

ESPN offers its one-hour show, "Nation's Business Today," over its cable net starting at 6:30 A.M. each weekday. Sponsored by the U.S. Chamber of Commerce, this program aims at the small business person rather than the investor.

RADIO PROSPERS WITH BUSINESS NEWS

Radio thrives on business news. FM stations usually feature music; AM features talk shows, a format ideal for business programs which answer viewers' questions.

About 120 stations around the country now offer talk and viewer-call shows. That doesn't sound like many, but they operate in major cities where millions of middle-aged and older people listen in. People over fifty-five years of age provide nearly two-thirds of the radio talk show audience and many of them either invest or worry enough about finance to seek radio advice.

KMNY (Money Radio) in Los Angeles operates twenty-four hours a day with business programs, some of which are now syndicated. Business News Broadcasting, a Boston, Massachusetts, company, and Business Radio Network, Inc., of Colorado Springs, Colorado, compete with KMNY to create nationwide networks of 'round-the-clock business news.

FNN operates in radio, too, with a service, *FNN Business News*. It provides thirty-two one-minute business-financial reports plus three two-minute regional reports daily to fifty stations. These cover 80 percent of the country's top fifty markets.

THE STAR BROADCASTERS

Paul Harvey, Bob Rosefsky, Bruce Williams, Bernard Meltzer, Bill Bresnan and a few others shine as stars year after year on the air. Generally, audiences are regional, but some personal finance jockeys like Williams dispense their advice through countrywide networks. Listeners regard them with the fervor displayed by disciples of bible belt television evangelists. Their audiences may top five million on shows which may run for three hours.

Question And Answer Time

Moderators glibly field telephone calls. They answer questions on any conceivable money subject, from home mortgage rates to stockbroker commissions and from tax interpretations to economic trends. Generally, though, they avoid strong recommendations, and they favor industries rather than specific companies.

A sampling of typical questions:

"My grandson will enter college in fourteen years and will need all the financial help he can get. How should I invest $10,000 now to best help him when he needs the money?"

"Should I finance a new home with a fixed or with a variable mortgage?"

"If IBM is so good, how come the stock isn't doing anything?"

"I bought an oil partnership last year for $10,000 and haven't received any income yet. Yesterday, a fellow from the company called and said they'd struck oil. Now, they want me to invest at least another $10,000 as my share for a development well which he says should return the $20,000 by at least five times. Does this sound good to you?"

A BROADENING ELECTRONIC WORLD

Developments come fast in today's electronic journalism. Television, cable and radio business news enterprises face an unsettled period as the communications industry works toward the electronic investment newsletter or even newspaper that might be carried via telephone lines to subscriber computers or fax machines. Network TV already seems resigned to focusing on entertainment. Cable encroaches upon the domain of telephone-computer financial news.

Televents Shows the Way

The Televents cable network provides an example of what may be in store for investors. In California, it now offers a $125 software package to its customers. This service links a computer to the cable and gives clients an array of investing programs. A touch of a keyboard automatically feeds data onto the computer's monitor and/or printer without affecting the television set's pictures.

The company offers the available services for $19.95 a month, after the one-time software cost. You pay the flat monthly rate regardless of how many hours on-line. With regular computer-phone systems, customers may encounter bills of several hundred dollars per month with heavy use.

With the Televents package, you can track personal investments, spot market trends, interest rates, commodities, currency exchange rates, leading indicators and mergers and acquisitions. Up-to-date national and international news keeps you abreast of events.

You can personalize the system with up to 128 stocks—a hefty portfolio, indeed. Meanwhile, you can get quotes and volume from major American and Canadian exchanges of all stocks at opening, midday and at close.

AT&T Challenges

Telephone companies, led by American Telephone & Telegraph, now seek authority to offer their services across the whole electronic field. AT&T's new glass fiber wires handle a thousand times more capacity than the copper wires currently in use in homes and businesses.

With operational freedom, your telephone company could bring you television entertainment, electronic catalogues for shopping, schedules from your local movie theatre, opera or concert hall and video telephones and computer connections to databases which literally could bring whole libraries into your home. Visual displays would appear on high-definition screens with resolution quality rivaling that in movie houses.

The Electronic Investment Letter

It doesn't take much imagination to see that this system also could carry electronic investment letters, placing all the world's markets at your fingertips. That exciting prospect may come in this decade.

If you receive Financial News Network on your television set, watch "The Wall Street Computer Review," a program which explores the fast-developing use of computers for investing. *Wall Street Computer Review* magazine and FNN co-produce the show (see Chapter 9 for more computer investing sources).

Chapter 7

Money-Making Newsletters

The standard investment newsletter dominates the dissemination of print financial news beyond that which comes in newspapers and magazines. Investors seek these letters for information to help them make money. They concentrate upon them with all the intensity evident in a story told by one peasant mule driver in the Elburz Mountains of Asia.

Iran's Shah still ruled from his palace in Tehran when a vacationing American diplomat hiked the slopes of 19,500-foot Mount Damavand north of the capital. The trails of the towering Elburz Range provide enough scenic views to please any mountain enthusiast, but this man remained a diplomat even when off duty.

Encountering a mule driver on a mountain trail, he engaged the gray-bearded native in a friendly conversation. Inevitably, he asked his favorite question for locals: Which country did Iranians like best, America, Britain or the Soviet Union?

The mule driver replied, in the indirect way of Iranians, that an old woman of a hundred years of age lived in his village. She had been married ten times and widowed each time. When villagers would ask her which husband she preferred, the woman would sigh and say: "God bless them all, they all wanted me for the same thing."

Ask a group of investors why they invest, and, initially, they too will probably settle on the same thing: to get rich. Query further,

and you find that goals diverge. One invests to send kids to college—certainly the antithesis of "getting rich." Another builds a retirement nest-egg. A couple wants a new home.

Still, money leads to those goals and its acquisition determines
success. Information which helps you acquire money is valuable,
even if you must pay for the advice. This fact has spawned a multi-
tude of investment letters, each dedicated to helping readers get
rich.

"Knowledge is of two kinds," said 18th Century lexicographer
Samuel Johnson. "We know a subject ourselves, or we know where
we can find information upon it." A good letter condenses profitable information which you don't know or perhaps only dimly realize. However, you must hunt among hundreds of them for the
good ones. They do exist, and this book will help you locate some of
them. Demand for profitable money advice always exceeds supply.

THE HISTORY OF ADVISORY LETTERS

As long as commerce has flowed, advisors have existed. Traders of
ancient Babylon and Carthage heeded reports from scouts in distant
lands concerning markets. In the 13th and 14th centuries A.D., Vene-
tian mariners wrote glowingly of Eastern voyages to attract money
for fresh ventures.

In old London, a small army of newsmongers developed in
neighborhood coffee shops after Sir Thomas Gresham established
Britain's Royal Exchange in 1566. (Monetary authorities still quote
his famous theorem, "bad money drives out the good.")

Over a century later, Daniel Defoe published a market letter little
remembered beside his novel, *Robinson Crusoe*. He invested in his
own South Sea Bubble recommendations and lost everything.

England's Industrial Revolution of 1769–1830 stimulated stock
and bond placements as factories, railroads and steamship lines
sought capital. A new investing class emerged, seeking more information about financial opportunities. The forerunners of today's investment letters developed to fill that need.

Following the British-American War of 1812 the Industrial Revolution jumped the Atlantic. The New York Stock and Exchange

Board opened in 1817 and ruled in 1819 that the exchange must conduct its business in secrecy. That "created the need for a new Wall Street industry—that of reporting hard-to-get financial news," writes Lloyd Wendt in his book, *The Wall Street Journal*. By the second half of the century, market letters had become an accepted part of the financial scene. As noted earlier, the *Journal* itself began as a market letter before evolving into a newspaper.

A CONFUSING FIELD

Money advisory letters come and go with stock market peaks and valleys. Today, the postal service delivers about 1,500 of them. However, they can't all be categorized easily. Should broker letters be counted? The *Merrill Lynch Market Letter*, Fidelity Investment's *The Independent Investor* or Schwab's *Insightful Investor* read as well as do many independent letters.

What about hobby letters? Collectors who invest in coins may perhaps read *The Coin Enthusiast's Journal*, but few would equate it, or trade and tax letters, with investors' letters. Yet, one like *Tax Hotline* may benefit your holdings. In the final analysis, anything that helps you make money is worth reading.

Investment letter guides will aid anyone searching for a good letter. About 200 investment letters form the nucleus of the field, with years of bear and bull market coverage behind them. These account for the bulk of newsletter circulation. Some of their authors become celebrities, develop a cult following and become investment gurus to subscribers.

Guides include: *The Individual Investor's Guide to Investment Publications* of International Publishing Corp. (sold by Probus Publishing Co., 118 N. Clinton St., Chicago, IL 60606, tele. 1-800/426-1520); *Investment Newsletter Directory*, Larimi Media Directories, a division of Billboard Publications, Inc., 1515 Broadway, New York, NY 10036, tele. 1-212/536-5266; *Investment Newsletters*, Public Relations Publishing Inc., 888 Seventh Ave., New York, NY 10106; and the *National Directory of Investment Newsletters*, Idea Publishing Corp., 55 E. Afton Ave., Yardley, PA 19067.

VARIETY OF LETTERS

Letters like *Indicator Digest* and *The Granville Market Letter* use technical data to analyze market moves. Others use fundamental information such as economic trends and company profits to tell their tale. Even more employ both to reach conclusions.

Letters may be weekly, biweekly, monthly or, in a few cases, quarterly. Prices range from low double figures to thousands of dollars for an annual subscription. They average around $150.

Many offer "hot lines," recorded phone messages which subscribers may tap. These reports, sometimes updated several times daily, serve investors who want data faster than Uncle Sam's mail provides.

For Gold Bugs And Nest Egg Builders

Letters cover every type of investment. Do you favor gold as the best hope against inflation? Then you might like Richard C. Young's *International Gold Report*, Adrian Day's *Investment Analyst* or James U. Blanchard's *Gold Newsletter*. *The Retirement Letter* aims at investors who build nest-eggs for their old age, or at retirees who must stretch their dollars.

For Conservative Investors

Standard & Poor's twelve-page *Outlook* caters to those who invest in major, solid companies. If you worry about your capital in this day of volatile markets, subscribe to a conservative letter like Charles Allmon's *Growth Stock Outlook*.

For International Investors

The *Outside Analyst* and the *Harry Schultz International Letter* take a global approach to investments. "Foreign markets can be profitable," says long-time money advisor Schultz.

For Speculators

The Option Advisor and the *Index Option Advisor* lead you through the perilous minefield of options trading. The *Short Alert* letter recommends stocks, but with a difference—it names market lemons for shorting. "Think negatively," says Roberto E. Veitia, the publisher.

For Risk-Takers

If you feel these risks can pay worthwhile returns, order Al Frank's *The Prudent Speculator*, which advocates margin trading. Frank, a one-time Las Vegas shill, has enough erudition to teach education at the University of California at Los Angeles and sufficient market savvy to generate profits from his methods.

For Capsulized Comments

If you prefer investment advice from a number of sources, take a look at the *Dick Davis Digest*. It distills investment thinking from 350 investment newsletters, then condenses that into twelve pages of readable information, along with thoughtful comments.

For Takeover Investors

If you like the profit opportunities of takeover situations, subscribe to Charles LaLoggia's *Special Situation Report*. He hunts for mergers before the deals develop, then names prospective companies, sometimes months ahead of actual transactions. Investors who invest early in deals make big money.

For Astral Tips

If you believe in astrology, an investment publication can serve you. The *Wall Street Astrologer*'s editors study planetary configurations to formulate their investing advice.

A Smorgasbord of Choices

Numerous narrow focus letters serve mutual fund investors (see Chapter 10), dealers in penny stocks or bidders for high technology shares. Others specifically cover bonds, precious metals, coins, currency trading, real estate investment trusts, closed-end securities, commodities, small company growth stocks, new stock issues and virtually any investment you can conceive.

LETTER SALES PITCHES

Investment advisors routinely employ a get-rich-quick sales theme. "DOUBLE OR TRIPLE YOUR MONEY IN JUST 2-3 YEARS WITH GUARANTEED U.S. TREASURIES!" blares a direct mail headline for Richard C. Young's 25,000-circulation *Intelligence Report*.

A brochure promoting *The Index Option Advisor* grows more extravagant. "You can make 40 times the profit of the best mutual funds, and you don't need to be an experienced trader or a wealthy investor to reap these huge profits—in bull and in bear markets," says Mary Lou Guidi, the publication's sales director.

Mark Skousen, the ex-CIA economist who edits *Forecasts & Strategies*, promises much if you subscribe to his letter. He pledges to explain "a unique opportunity to make 100% in gold, even if the price of gold goes nowhere; a tax-free zero coupon bond that's guaranteed to give you a remarkable 8-to-1 return; and an exceptional opportunity to make 100%-300% a year by acquiring founder's stock in promising young companies."

In justice to Skousen, he did warn subscribers to quit the market in 1987 weeks before The Crash. Few others did.

Skousen's merchandising pales beside the promises of *World Market Perspective*. One of its ads reads: "HOW TO TURN $250 INTO $51,888 in four years or less." Impatient investors might regard four years as a long time for getting rich, but one shouldn't quibble over a profit of 5,164 percent a year.

Read on, and it grows better. Literature promises a batch of moneymaking investing brochures with the subscription. One describes how you can earn big profits on *no investment at all*. How? Well, the ad states right there in black and white that you can borrow money from banks at one rate and redeposit the money in the same place for higher interest.

"For example," claims the ad, "now you can borrow from some of the world's largest banks at 7% and redeposit with the same bank at the same branch for 12%. You earn a cool 5% for doing absolutely nothing."

Unfortunately, the ad names no institutions in the copy. Could they be among those savings and loans which lost hundreds of billions in 1988-1990? If only *World Market Perspective* included a name, you could request a checking account there. Then you could write a check to the publication for the $99 subscription and you would not be out a dime.

A Cautionary Warning

If all this sounds too good to be true, you possess acute perception. Many letters certainly can help you make money. Many, though, oversell with their glowing promises. Charles Allmon, editor of *Growth Stock Outlook*, frowns at such tactics. "If you want a letter, pick a long-established one with a record you can check," he recommends. (That could be viewed as promotional, too, though it is still low-key for money advisors. Allmon's letter ranks among the oldest in the business, with a profitable history which can be verified easily.)

THE GLOOM AND DOOMERS

Another form of exaggeration appears in newsletter promotions. When not promising you boundless prosperity, advisors scare you silly with their sales offerings.

"I've never been more scared in my life. Most people are totally unaware of the investing dangers ahead," says Howard Ruff in direct mail plugs for his *Ruff Times* letter. He foresees a "deep recession" leading to a depression. His letter can save you from financial ruin, he claims.

The Debt Burden

Predictions forecasts the future more dramatically. "Public and private debt is so high it will never be paid off," warns Lee Euler, publisher. "When the next crash comes, this immense debt will act like a lead weight around a swimmer's ankles. Thousands of corporations will sink like rocks dropped off a pier."

You can protect your capital and avoid the catastrophe, however, by subscribing, the mailer promises. With help of twenty-six super investment advisors, the publication will steer you to a safe financial port.

The Collapse of Everything

A mailer for Doug Casey's *Investing in Crisis* sees crises in all directions. It says: "People who have some savings and are counting on mutual funds, passbook accounts or the equity in their homes are going to be in for most unpleasant surprises."

Like what? The copy answers that question.

Real estate prices will collapse. Inflation will reach record proportions. The long-term bond market will cease to exist. Banks and money funds will become precarious places for your money.

Again, a sliver of hope exists if you subscribe.

Is It The End Of The World?

A full-page advertisement for John King's *Future Economic Trends* reaches the height—or is it the depth?—of pessimism. "THE DOW JONES WILL CRASH TO 41," the headline shouts. The copy reads: "Interest rates will soar, the Prime Rate reaching 35%. Gold will surpass $1,800 an ounce, silver $120 an ounce. Real estate will fall to perhaps one cent on the dollar. Oil will fall from $20 to $10 a barrel, then $9, then $5, Then $3, and finally, to 25 cents a barrel. The Dow Jones Average will retrace its historic low average of 41 (in September, 1933)."

Wait! Don't take poison just yet. Subscribe to King's publication and "you will get a great deal of practical information on preparing for and surviving the coming crash," the ad promises.

Admittedly, America faces problems with deficits in trade and in the budget, corporations and consumers deeply in debt and the dollar below its value of the early 1980s. However, America possesses basic strengths which pessimists don't recognize. In the past, this country surmounted worse troubles than those facing us today. So don't be overwhelmed by either the pessimism or by the lurid promises of quick riches. Be cautious with your money, but don't panic.

THE RECENT HISTORY OF NEWSLETTERS

Part of the fear expressed by some newsletters today stems from their own panic at declining circulations. This comes after the letter industry's biggest boom in history.

The advisory letter business benefited substantially from the growth in recent years of desktop publishing—the use of computers to replace print shops. This slashed entry costs for embryo letters. Subsequently, the boom stock years following 1982 saw letters proliferate and circulation soar.

Then came the October, 1987, market crash. This hit investment letters hard, as did increases in postage rates. Circulation declined, promotion costs mounted and about 250 letters folded.

A Relative Recession, for Some

Howard Ruff, the ex-professional singer and super-salesman owner of *The Ruff Times* letter, claimed a circulation of 175,000 in 1984. Today he reports a rather loose subscription figure of "over a hundred thousand." Don't be misled by his tale of hard times, however. Once circulation of a letter passes 1,000, costs drop sharply. With a smooth-running operation, net profit may total half of the gross. So there are numerous self-made multi-millionaires among investment letter writers, including Ruff.

Richard E. Band, ex-editor of *Personal Finance*, says: "During the halcyon days of the newsletter industry in 1983 and 1984, our circulation peaked at 240,000. However, even with today's subscriber base [86,000], the letter is quite profitable." Band now edits *Profit-able Investing* letter.

The late Arnold Bernhard, a genius in stock analysis and creator of the *Value Line Survey*, left an estimated fortune of $390 million when he died in 1987 high on the *Forbes* 400. Nobody else in the letter field has managed to make that list, but then Bernhard's career spanned well over a half century.

Success breeds success in investing. Look to investment advisors with deep pockets when selecting investment letters. Financial advice merits little attention if the donor shows no benefit from it.

THE LETTER WRITERS

Most letters start as solo operations in a home office, perhaps on the kitchen table. Sometimes, the writer previously worked as a stockbroker. Success at personal investing may have led to advising others. However, no particular career leads to letter production.

Joseph Granville and James Dines, legends in this field, worked as brokers. Granville wrote a financial bestseller in 1960, launched the *Granville Market Letter* in its afterglow. Harry Browne followed the same bestseller route to his letter, *Harry Browne's Special Reports*. Tom Holt, co-editor of *Holt Advisory*, immigrated from China and learned investing in libraries.

The entertainment field supplies its quota of writers, probably because showmanship helps sell anything. Samson Coslow, creator of *Indicator Digest*, wrote popular songs before turning to a career in finance.

The Ney Report comes from actor-author Richard Ney, co-star with Greer Garson in the movie "Mrs. Miniver," and her real-life husband for a time. Robert Prechter, editor of *Elliott Wave Theorist*, played in a dance band, a humble start for the producer of a letter which grossed $4 million annually during the bull market.

To succeed, letter writers must convince potential readers of their oracular talents. This takes hard selling. Moreover, self-promotion must be permanent.

Oscar Wilde (1854–1900), the Irish playwright and wit, once wrote: "There is only one thing in the world worse than being talked about, and that is not being talked about." Letter writers agree. They show irritation when criticized, yet they fear being ignored. So they promote themselves diligently.

Donoghue, a Man Seldom Unseen

William E. Donoghue, a bearded, aggressive man of forty-nine, publishes two letters, *Donoghue's Moneyletter* and *Donoghue's Money Fund Report*. He also knows how to attract attention. At sedate finance conferences, he wears a trim, white suit which makes him easy to locate. Why white? "To show everyone I'm one of the good guys," he says.

If you miss him inside, you might notice him in the convention center parking lot. He drives a blood-red Jaguar sedan, with an engine that outroars a fire truck. At one investment seminar, the moderator introduced him as "a man unburdened by false modesty." Donoghue grinned and nodded.

Over 1,000 institutions subscribe to Donoghue's money fund letter. His business grosses $2.5 million annually and he looks as if he can afford a closet full of white suits, plus a fleet of Jaguars.

Such *savoir faire* appeals to readers of investment letters. You wouldn't accept financial advice from somebody who looks shabby, would you? Of course, behind the flashy front, a writer needs a satisfactory product and Donoghue has mastered the formula.

Ruff, a One-Man Industry

Howard Ruff, a professional singer after college, honed his market knowledge as a broker. He remains a super salesman rather than a literary star.

As a young and fairly successful professional singer, he appeared a couple times on "The Ed Sullivan Show" and with the Philadelphia Symphony under the baton of Eugene Ormandy. He found his real career after working as a broker and failing in business. He became a counselor to the thousands of little investors who need advice concerning how to succeed.

Today, he says: "I am the financial advisor to America's neglected and abused middle class."

A Mormon elder, he remains "the ultimate Boy Scout," ever ready to wave the flag and to stand solidly behind God and country. Above all, he is a salesman

"I'm a pretty darn good marketer," he says, in the strongest language he ever uses. "My newsletter's circulation didn't come by accident. When you invent a better mousetrap, the world does not beat a path to your door unless you develop ways of inducing people to try it."

In folksy manner, Ruff reports in *Ruff Times* on his wife, his thirteen kids (four adopted), his seventeen grandchildren and his Labrador, Sassie. Eventually, he writes about the market, rails against inflation and suggests ways to beat it. He likes some gold in every portfolio, especially when he grows pessimistic. His investment philosophy is reflected in his letter's title. He launched the biweekly in 1975 when the Vietnamese War was creating much trouble for this country.

However, Ruff disliked the "gloom and doom" title the press hung on him and he grew uncomfortable with the letter's title as the Reagan Administration took office. In 1982, he renamed it the *Financial Success Report*, and its tone brightened. As Reagan spending raised inflation threats, the gloom reappeared. In October 1986, he returned to the *Ruff Times* title.

Meet Joseph Granville

Joseph Granville also believes that Broadway histrionics accelerate the march to the promised land. Once he concealed planks beneath swimming pool waters at an Arizona resort hosting an investment meet. Then he "walked on water," as followers cheered. The unspoken promotional message reached investors: anybody who can imitate Christ should be able to tell you which stocks to buy and when.

The ebullient Granville is old enough for Medicare, as his lean countenance reveals. But he seldom acts like a grandfather. He appeared once at a money conference with a pet chimpanzee as his guest. He named the animal Dwarfman to needle columnist Dan Dorfman, with whom Granville was feuding at the time.

Another time, at Atlantic City waiters transported Granville to the podium as he lay in a coffin, ticker tape streaming behind him.

The promotional message here escaped most of the onlookers, but one of his worshipful subscribers in attendance was heard to say: "That's just like Joe."

Indeed, it was.

It is sometimes said that a person will stand on his or her head to get attention. Granville did just that—literally, not figuratively—in one hotel lobby. His act riveted the eyes of everybody around. However, none of his antics has detracted a bit from his letter's circulation: at its peak, it had 15,000 subscribers waiting eagerly for his messages.

His subscribers abandoned him in a rush, however, when he woefully missed a major bull market. Sell everything, he advised, before that August, 1982, upsurge. He continued bearish as the market climbed. Circulation of the *Granville Market Letter* collapsed to about 900 in inverse proportion to the market rise. Granville, though, rallied with a stream of sharp stock calls to claim a circulation of about 5,000 in 1989.

The Daddy Warbucks of Letter Writers

Harry Schultz, editor of *The International Harry Schultz Letter*, is too dignified to stand on his head. Yet he promotes himself as well or better than anybody else in the field. After *The Guinness Book of World Records* named him "the world's most expensive investment advisor," he added that title to his promotional lexicon.

People who read his letters hang on every word. Once when he held a seminar of his subscribers in London, the city's newspapers termed the affair "The Billion Dollar Meet." In addition to writing his letter, he charges a consulting fee of $2,400 an hour for explaining how you, too, might reach his lofty financial plane ($3,400 an hour on weekends).

FEMALE INVESTMENT ADVISORS

The few women in the field of investment newsletters attract attention just by being females—they need not stand on their heads to stand out.

Financial publications frequently mention Geraldine Weiss because of her astute recommendations in her letter, *Investment Quality Trends*. The Aden sisters, Mary Ann and Pamela, acquired fame with their prescient calls concerning gold. They now publish a letter, *The Aden Analysis*, which is building a following.

The Boss At Value Line

Value Line, an institution in investing, takes its direction from 54-year-old Jean Bernhard Buttner. Her estimated net worth is $315 million. She inherited her job from her father, the firm's founder, and benefited from his tutelage. Now she commands the ship at *Value Line*. Revenues totaled $74.7 million in fiscal 1988, making the firm a leader in the money advisory field. The company does not publicize circulation of its flagship *Value Line Survey*. *The Wall Street Journal* cited a figure of 91,800 for 1988; another publication estimated it at 200,000 in 1990. Today's actual figure probably lies in between.

MONEY ADVISORS EXPAND ACTIVITIES

Investment letter writers broaden activities as new avenues appear. Some manage your money directly. Usually they accept only $100,000 or more for management, or they create mutual funds tailored to their investing concepts. A few sell products, coins, precious metals and such, as well as advice.

They also write investment books and pamphlets, create videos and tapes and sell marketing strategies. Publishing companies blossom behind them. They speak at seminars. Stars collect over $5,000 for an appearance. A few become television and radio personalities. The superstars promote their own profitable seminars. Some letters have developed into mini-conglomerates.

NEWSLETTER EMPIRES

Value Line merits this designation. Other empires in the letter business include Target, Inc. (the parent company of *Ruff Times*), KCI

Communications, Phillips Publishing Inc., Standard & Poor's, the Institute for Econometric Research, the American Media Group, Inc. and the National Institute of Business Management (NIBM).

Commerce Clearing House also ranks as an important financial services firm but it publishes no investment letter, unless you consider the *Pink Sheets* of its National Quotation Bureau as such.

The National Institute of Business Management (NIBM)

NIBM's name sometimes creates confusion. "We are a for-profit company, not a trade association," says Paul Hencke, editor in chief of NIBM. One division produces newsletters, with the *Executive Wealth Advisory* the key investment periodical. A second division sells management information, business, tax and special letters, planning reports and such.

Adds Hencke: "NIBM has been around over fifty years and enjoys a high degree of loyalty in its circulation base of about 500,000."

Phillips Publishing

This Potomac, Maryland, firm has also built a reputation for itself as a letter business giant. Its investing publications include *Forecasts & Strategies*, the *International Gold Fund Report*, *Mutual Fund Investing*, *Profitable Investing*, *The Retirement Letter* and *Young's Intelligence Report*. It also publishes letters in the medical, health and other areas.

The Institute for Econometric Research

Here Norman Fosback holds forth. Its research serves over 250,000 investors. It publishes *Income and Safety*, *The Insiders*, *Market Logic*, *Mutual Fund Forecaster* and *New Issues*. The Institute claims that *Mutual Fund Forecaster* now has the largest circulation of any financial advisory letter in the world.

KCI Communications

This company publishes *Personal Finance,* one of the most profitable of the investing letters. It also publishes *Investment Monthly, MJF Growth Stock Advisory* and *The Utility Forecaster,* as well as investing studies. It sells a 119-page *Investor's Guide to Bonds* and a list of the best bond plays for the 1990s. It has a score of other investing titles.

The American Media Group

The American Media Group publishes numerous letters of different kinds, three of them for investing: *Growth Stock Report, Oakley's Aggressive Stock Alert* and *Personal Investing News.*

Jim Blanchard's Enterprises

James U. Blanchard III created his own little empire in New Orleans. Every fall, he produces a major investment seminar in the city. He publishes the *Gold Newsletter,* a mini-magazine on coins entitled *Blanchard's American Rarities* and special reports on personal investing. He pioneered the asset allocation mutual fund, and now has an interest in the Blanchard Group of Mutual Funds, which manages $405 million.

His company cooperated with the U.S. Postal Service and the Consumer Information Center to produce the 40-page booklet, *A Consumer's Guide to Coin Investment* (write CIC for free copy, address in appendix). He built a coin business with an annual volume of $100 million when it was sold to a unit of General Electric Capital Corp. He still dabbles in coins.

Yet he remains low-key in an industry given to hype. He says, "Coins aren't designed to be speculative vehicles delivering a quick profit. I advise clients to hold any coin for at least three to five years and preferably a decade or more."

Standard & Poor's

Most investors know Standard & Poor's from its market guides described earlier and from its S&P 500 Index. It also publishes two successful letters, *The Outlook* and *Emerging & Special Situations* plus investing guides such as *Mutual Fund Profiles*, S&P must be included among majors in the money advisory field.

Moody's Services, another financial publications giant, is not a factor in the advisory letter field.

ODDBALL LETTERS

Market letters have become increasingly difficult to classify. Take *Market Express*, for instance, one of several publications from WMP Enterprises in Orlando, Florida. "This is not a newspaper, not a magazine, not a newsletter in any ordinary sense," says Roberto E. Veitia, its publisher. It recommends computer-selected stock buys via Priority Mail to subscribers.

The company also publishes the letters *The International Advisor* and *Short Alert*, plus the tabloid *MoneyWorld*. The latter looks like *Barron's* with color typography, and reads like a magazine. Unlike investment letters, it carries advertisements, usually of coin or precious metals merchandisers.

Very similar in appearance and tone is the *Personal Investing News*, which also carries financial advertising. News columns frequently contain market predictions from well-known letter producers. This includes the likes of Charles Allmon, James McKeever, Martin Zweig, Howard Ruff, Robert Prechter and others.

ELECTRONIC PUBLISHING

Electronic distribution has also broadened opportunities for investment letter producers. *Market Fax, The Granville Letter* and others now reach subscribers through fax machines. "This service is what your fax is for," claims a *Market Fax* promotion. Expect more such letters to emerge as the fax machine becomes as popular as a phone.

Telephone letters, such as *Stock Market Hotline*, operate like the "hot lines" maintained by many letter editors. However, no printed copy at all comes with the service, just articulated data about the market.

AUDIO CASSETTE LETTERS

The audio cassette finds uses among investment advisors, too. *Investor's Hotline,* for instance, dispatches at least twelve topical ninety-minute tapes a year to subscribers. Each tape contains four interviews with market letter writers like Robert Prechter, Bert Dohmen-Ramirez, Mark Skousen, Dick Fabian, Doug Casey, Charles Allmon, William Donoghue and others, or with financial authorities like Kurt Richebacher, one time managing director of Germany's Deutche Bank, and John Templeton, the money guru.

COMPUTER LETTERS

Computers continue to open new vistas in the investing letter field. You can't even subscribe to *The Princeton Portfolios* unless you possess a computer and a modem. The letter is entirely electronic. The subject of computers will be discussed further in Chapter 9, which also provides an analysis of the many technical informational sources now available for managing your portfolio.

The investment letter business indeed does broaden your informational avenues. But keep this in the proper perspective: letters which fit your personality and risk patterns may make you a better investor, but they cannot transform you into a profit maker if you can't balance a checkbook, let alone manage a portfolio.

There is an old joke about a man who breaks his arm. A doctor sets the break in a cast, and assures the man that everything should be all right. The patient asks the doctor if he will be able to play the violin when the cast is removed.

"Sure thing," says the doctor, "perfectly."

"Wonderful," says the man. "I couldn't play a note before I broke my arm."

Financial advisors *can* help you with your investment problems. They *cannot* convert you into a financial genius if you haven't displayed much talent for it previously. They may one day show you how to recognize a new Wal-Mart or an Apple Computer when it struggles for recognition. Investors grow rich with such finds.

Chapter 8

Fundamental Analysis Pays Off

Sears, Roebuck & Co. built the world's tallest skyscraper to house its staff of 8,000. The 102-floor Sears Tower rises over Chicago's Loop—a giant monument, but not to the company's success.

Wal-Mart Stores, Inc., another big merchandiser, quarters its lean staff in a modest, three-story building in Bentonville, Arkansas. It prefers sales to monuments.

In the last decade, Sears' retail sales climbed from $17.5 billion to an estimated $58 billion in 1989. Wal-Mart's turnover soared from $1.2 billion to an estimated $26.7 billion. Sears stock doubled in price in that time, but Wal-Mart's share value skyrocketed by *thirty-six* times.

When you invest in stock, you seek companies that will really pay off, like Wal-Mart. You might one day collect $36 for each $1 invested in stocks, too, but acting alone, you must study much stock information to find such winners. Investment letters focus your search, provide advice and interpret the available data. A financial newspaper or magazine might do the same, but letters tailor their copy much more specifically. Of letter writers who employ fundamental analysis, the better ones speak in a language which you can understand.

WHAT INVESTMENT LETTERS DO

The editors of investment letters interview the management of companies you might not know exist. They subscribe to obtuse trade publications as well as standbys like *The Wall Street Journal*. They search for companies with robust earnings trends, a high return on equity, strong managements and products or services in demand.

The *California Technology Stock Letter*, a San Francisco-based computer industry biweekly, illustrates how such a letter functions. Lissa Morgenthaler, one of its editors, says: "We're right here in Silicon Valley where much of the news and wealth of the computer industry is made. To get information, we visit companies, competitors, suppliers and customers. We go to trade shows, seminars and product announcements."

You probably do not have the time or business connections to call on companies. Letter editors do. Moreover, the good ones also possess the ability to interpret their findings. Explains Ms. Morgenthaler: "After reporting, we tell you what's going on, in layman's language. We describe each technology, tell you what is of investment significance, and give you specific buys and sells, with buy limits and target prices."

Helpful Supplemental Sources

If you don't understand the terminology of investment letters, buy a copy of *Money's Complete Guide to Personal Finance and Investment Terms* (Barron's Educational Series, Inc., 113 Crossways Park Drive, Woodbury, NY 11797 or bookstores). This work defines over 2,500 financial terms from "ABC Agreement" to "Zeros."

Sales, earnings, book value and balance sheet data appear in a company's annual report. Public companies want people to buy their stocks, so they freely mail yearly statements to outsiders. If you can't read an annual report, obtain a copy of Merrill Lynch's free, thirty-page *How to Read a Financial Report*. Explanations clarify net fixed assets, accrued expenses, capital stock and the other arcane terms which accountants prefer.

A handy aid for the individual investor which can be found in most libraries is the *Value Line Survey*. *The Wall Street Journal* calls it "a virtual bible of stock-researching information for small investors."

In 1990, a three-month trial subscription to the *Survey* cost $60, a bargain if it helps you locate just one hot stock pick. A copy of *Value Line Methods of Evaluating Common Stocks* comes with the subscription. First written by the firm's late founder, Arnold Bernhard, it not only explains how to use the *Survey*, but it also provides insights into fundamental analysis in general. This could be your correspondence course into the topic.

Standard & Poor's *Stock Reports* rivals *Value Line* with its data, but it costs nearly twice as much as the *Survey* and sells mainly to corporate rather than individual investors. Pay attention, too, to well-known fundamentalist investors like Warren Buffett, Mario Gabelli, John Templeton and others. They can give you ideas without any statistical gibberish.

MEET FUNDAMENTALIST CHARLES ALLMON

Charles Allmon, a dean of fundamental letter writers says: "We're talking to managers of companies all the time. Then, we pass worthwhile information to our readers."

Why should you listen to someone like Allmon? As a money manager, he controls nearly a half billion dollars, with a record of fifteen consecutive years of gains. He succeeds because he locates those Wal-Mart type stocks before they become well known. In one of many like cases, he advised readers to buy Wallace Computer Services in 1975 when the stock sold at a little over $2 a share (considering splits). It sold for fifteen times that figure in 1990.

As a letter writer, he tells it like it is, so perhaps you can adapt his investing philosophies to make big money for yourself. His semi-monthly *Growth Stock Outlook* letter focuses upon attractive, fast-growing companies, the type which earn hefty payoffs when you hit a winner.

Growth Stock Outlook *Described*

The letter usually runs eight pages. Page one contains Allmon's
views about the market. Once a month he shows the standing of his
$50,000 portfolio (established 6/27/1973), worth $612,475 in August, 1990 for a 1,125 percent gain. He held 90 percent in cash, re-
flecting his concern about the stock market.

The letter offers readers late company news along with Allmon's
comments. Every other issue carries a six-page list of the better
stocks currently followed by his service. This includes forty-three
New York Stock Exchange, nine American Stock Exchange and
forty-seven over-the-counter stocks. The list contains key statistics—
P/E, price, book value, return on equity, years of growth, and so
on. "A" ratings mark his top choices. His star Big Board shares in
1990 included American Family, American International Group,
Carter-Wallace, Clayton Homes, Clorox, Ennis Business Forms,
Hershey Foods, Jostens, Longs Drugs, New Plan Realty Trust, Uni-
First Corp. UST, Inc. and Zero Corp.

Only one American Stock Exchange company, Hipotronics, rated
an "A." Sixteen of Allmon's forty-seven over-the-counter issues
held it.

Allmon's Background

Allmon is a feisty one-time *National Geographic* writer-photographer
who made so much money investing while covering the globe that
friends sought his advice. Allmon eventually found investment advising more alluring than journalism, became a full-time money
manager, then launched his letter in 1965.

He now occupies a Bethesda, Maryland, office adorned with pictures of his travels in seventy countries. He often tours the country
to speak at investment meetings, appear on television or radio
shows or interview corporate managers. He has lectured on investing at the Harvard University Business School, the Wharton School
of the University of Pennsylvania and Yale University's Business
Forum.

A Voice In The Money Media

Allmon can be heard on the Financial News Network every Tuesday morning for a live five-minute interview at 1:30 P.M. Eastern time. Just about every major business and financial publication featured him at various times, including the likes of *The Wall Street Journal*, *Forbes*, the *New York Times* and *Money* magazine. Investment seminar promoters like him on platforms because he speaks frankly and may tromp verbally on exposed toes. So he draws crowds.

His Investing Philosophy

Allmon advises diversification in a portfolio to spread the risks. He believes in buying and holding if fundamentals fit his formula. Sooner or later the market recognizes the favorable picture and the stock's price rises, he says.

He detests technical analysis, equates technicians with carnival fortune tellers. "We do not use charts," he says. "If I did, I wouldn't be talking to you because we would not have a track record. We would be like every other technician, losing money."

He adds: "Book value and dividend yield are the two best measures for the investor."

How Allmon Selects Stocks

"Our objective is to double each stock's listing price in five years," says he. Normally, a company must show a minimum 17 percent annual growth rate compounded for four years for its stock to qualify as a buy or hold.

He also wants low or non-existent institutional holdings (pension funds, college endowment funds, trust accounts and so on) in the company. Institutions invest or disinvest with a herd instinct that spells disaster should all depart *en masse* from a small company's stock. Price falls of 40 or 50 percent may occur, sometimes in one day.

Allmon likes a price-to-sales ratio of under one. Thus, a company with a $20 stock price needs sales exceeding $20 per share to interest him. With a million common shares outstanding, sales should exceed $20 million annually to fit his pattern.

He then sketches a stock evaluation formula worth your attention when culling stocks. Companies should have a sales growth of 15 to 20 percent a year, a history of growing earnings and a return on stockholders' equity of 17 to 25 percent. The price should not exceed 1.3 or 1.4 times book value, with low debt (10 to 15 percent debt to equity). Balance sheets must be strong (current assets 2.5-4 to 1 over current liabilities).

In 1990, his model portfolio (real, not imagined) included J.M. Smucker, bought in 1982 at $13.13 and then selling for over $70; Standard Register, a $5.87 stock in 1983, worth three times that in 1989; and Ennis Business forms, acquired for $8.81 a share in 1985, worth triple that today.

Law Of Compound Interest Explained

"We fell in love with the law of compound interest many years ago," says Allmon. "In this business, the tortoise usually beats the hare and patience sometimes is worth more than money."

The law of compound interest simply means that money works for you when you reinvest dividends or interest in a compound account. You earn interest on interest and/or dividends, then more interest on that and so on. Even a few years with that law on your side puts you on the road to financial independence.

Use the Rule of 72 if you want to estimate how long it will take to double your money with compound interest. Divide 72 by the interest figure and you get the number of years for doubling. As an example, in early 1989 you could obtain a guaranteed 9.5 percent return in several safe investment. Divide 72 by 9.5. You will double your money in 7.6 years at that interest rate.

If you invest $1,000 in a compound interest reinvestment plan without making any subsequent deposits you will earn:

Year	9.5%	12%	15%
1	$1,095	$1,120	$1,150
5	1,574	1,762	2,011
10	2,478	3,106	4,046
20	6,142	3,106	16,366

COMPREHENDING FUNDAMENTAL INFORMATION

The average investor finds fundamental data easier to understand than the specialized language of the technician. Still, some eyes may glaze at the constant references to price/earnings, cash flow and such, with numbers interspersed amid data.

You subscribe to one or more investment letters of your choice mainly to obtain interpretations of all that data. The good letter interprets the data for you. If you prefer doing your own analysis, your library may save you a few dollars, your broker may explain some facets of the data and you always have access to company annual and quarterly reports.

For 1,700 companies, the already mentioned *Value Line* offers in its Ratings & Reports section all the information mentioned in Allmon's or any other fundamentalist's formula. Once you have the vital information, you can develop a strategy of your own to fit your circumstances.

Generally, fundamental investors do not operate as market timers, since most take a long-term view of markets. The market timer abandons positions in slumps (hopefully just before) to return in bull markets (again hopefully just before). Fundamentalists insist that nobody can predict market swings. (In the next chapter, a few market timers will have their say.)

VALUE INVESTING

Benjamin Graham (1894-1976) a money manager and university finance professor, deserves credit for categorizing and amplifying the "value approach" in fundamental investing. This investing strategy, well liked by Mario Gabelli, Walter Buffett and others, seeks to digest statistics to formulate a "value" for a stock. If the share sells well below that figure, value investors buy it to hold until the market price catches up with the true value.

In 1934, Graham collaborated with Columbia University professor David L. Dodd to write *Security Analysis*, a finance industry classic. It became a textbook at universities. (McGraw-Hill offers an updated version—call 1-800-2-MCGRAW to order via charge card.)

In 1949, Graham wrote a more understandable sequel for laymen entitled *The Intelligent Investor*. This book provides invaluable background for your fundamental investing career. Your library might still have a copy available.

A Value Newsletter

Al Frank, editor of *The Prudent Speculator*, assiduously searches for undervalued shares. He puts his money where his mouth is, investing his own money in a personal portfolio followed in each issue of his letter, published every three weeks. Frank employs margin to enhance his gains when he feels bullish.

"My approach is to find stocks trading at bargain levels according to their fundamental valuations," says Frank. "These undervalued stocks, whether small capitalization or big cap, are out of favor and their fundamental values haven't been recognized in the market place." That term "small cap" generally means a company with a capitalization (value of all stock outstanding) totaling less than $200 to $300 million.

Frank buys stocks rather than the market. He does not move in and out with reckless abandon with each rise or fall of stock indices. He buys and holds, and he will wait for years if necessary for an undervalued stock to rise to its true value.

Other Fundamental Letters

The fundamental approach serves well for locating growth companies on their way up. *BI Research, Emerging & Special Situations, Market Mania, Kenneth J. Gerbino Investment Letter* and *OTC Insight* employ it to locate stocks. Sometimes the special situations involve the restructure of fairly large companies; at other times letters spotlight tiny, new corporations.

FUNDAMENTAL STOCK APPLICATIONS

BI Research operates in a more adventurous style than most, recommending companies just learning to walk. *Market Mania*, too, names little-known stocks for consideration. With such shares, buyers often must hold shares awhile for the promise to materialize. It may not. When it does, you are likely to score big.

With small capitalization stocks, investors must diversify, buying several stocks at a time to spread the risks, even if this means small holdings of each. Investing assistance for this strategy is hard to find. *Value Line* covers few companies on the over-the-counter market and none among penny stocks, so it offers no assistance for the evaluation of most small shares. *Growth Stock Outlook* sends its special quarterlies *Junior Growth Stocks* and *New Issues Digest* with its regular subscription. This includes statistical data on some of them.

Sources mentioned earlier in Chapter 3 in connection with penny stocks could help. So might the magazine *OTC Review* and letters such as *OTC Insight, OTC Review, Special Situations, The Acker Letter* and *MPT Review*.

When dealing in shares of very small companies, however, you learn early that good statistical data may be difficult to acquire. Moreover, a company that is only an idea possesses no record to create any statistics. That might be a good argument for avoiding them, but such avoidance prevents you from ever acquiring some embryo Wal-Mart at $1 a share to sell later at $40 each.

Investment Horizons, edited by Gerald Perritt, favors small company stocks. Perritt urges mutual fund investors to seek vehicles which put their money into such companies. Look for a fund that manages $100 million or less in assets, he advises—a money manager finds it easier to handle a fund that size, rather than a larger one.

Dividend Investing

Conservative fundamentalists might profit by following the strategy of Geraldine Weiss, editor of the semimonthly *Investment Quality Trends*. She likes dividend paying companies, the higher the return the better, provided strength lies under earnings.

With this technique, you hold a portfolio of high dividend companies. If a stock with a better dividend and a rising profit trend appears on your horizon as one of your companies slips, you sell the poor performer and buy the better payer.

"Rising dividends not only provide increased income, allowing stockholders to keep pace with inflation, they also support stock prices and increase stock values," contends Ms. Weiss. Her letter tracks 350 blue chip stocks and steers readers to the best buys.

Conservative investors love dividends. They realize accountants often manipulate statistics to improve reports. But companies need hard cash to pay dividends. Ready money almost always beats an accountant's shadow "profits," allegedly payable through stock appreciation at an unspecified time in the distant future.

One fundamentalist technique calls for holding the top five dividend payers among the thirty shares in the Dow Jones Industrial Index. The investor adjusts portfolios once or twice a year. If a new share pushes into the group, the investor sells the lowest paying of the six and switches those funds into the new stock.

A variation of the technique builds a portfolio from shares of companies which increased their cash dividends every year for at least the last ten. Stocks in that group include: Allegheny Power, Bristol-Myers, Citicorp, Emerson Electric, First Interstate Bancorp, Humana, Johnson & Johnson, J.P. Morgan, National Medical Enterprise, San Diego Gas & Electric, Security Pacific Corp. and numerous others. Should a company fail to hike its dividend, the investor sells, and buys another star.

Conserving Your Capital

Executive Wealth Advisory, a National Institute of Business Management fundamental publication, appears semimonthly. It covers an array of investment topics ranging from bonds to real estate. A few of its articles include: "The best limited partnerships"; "Buying a home"; "Why a Keogh is too good to pass up"; "Year-end tax planning guide"; "Money trends, playing the yield curve"; and "Retirement money."

Editor Philip Springer summarizes the economic or market outlook on the first of its eight pages. The lead article features such topics as opportunities in foreign stocks or recommendations among growth shares. It could contain tips about bond selection or about what to avoid when investing. Editors stress the conserving of capital and often interview successful money managers to support the letter's investment philosophy.

More of the "Safe" Approach

Harry Browne's Special Reports aims at protecting your capital, too. Browne, a popular figure at money conferences, advocates maintaining a hard core of super-safe investments in portfolios. Carefully select these to provide financial protection in any sort of economic climate, he recommends.

You may be a little more speculative with the rest of your portfolio, according to his investing techniques. However, his letter will not prod you into wild chases for quick profits, for he knows that such gains require foolhardy risks.

The Contrarian Approach

Personal Finance presents fundamental data laced with technical support. Its editors handle the eight-page publication with a maverick approach, that of avowed market "contrarians."

This type of investor realizes that mob psychology moves markets. Crowds grow irrational and may rush along with the flow, whichever way that is. In a bull market, people swarm into stocks because everybody else does. They bid stock prices much higher than actual valuations.

Then comes a crash. Stock prices tumble; pessimism dominates. Few buyers appear, except for contrarians. To illustrate, one editor quotes the late billionaire J. Paul Getty: "Buy when everyone else is selling, and hold until everyone else is buying."

Contrarians formulate opinions by studying the sentiment surveys of such publications as *Investors Intelligence*. This investment letter periodically polls scores of other letter editors to gauge their bullishness or bearishness.

Most contrarians apply their philosophy only to stocks. Editors believe it works in real estate, bonds, precious metals, commodities and collectibles, as well as stocks. Thus, the letter covers numerous kinds of investments, but only when editors see profit potentials or when major pitfalls appear. They usually recommend investing long, only occasionally advising shorting.

They edit the publication like a magazine, welcoming contributions from outside authorities. When Al Frank wrote a piece about small company stocks for *Personal Finance*, an editor injected an introductory paragraph: "Al Frank has one of the finest long-term records of any stock picker in the business. *The Prudent Speculator* chalked up an amazing total return of 303% in the eight years ended June 30, 1988."

A "Capsule Advisory" page reports what other advisory letters say, with endorsements or criticisms. From *Staton's Stock Market Advisory* an editor culls the line: "Yield curve inversions either slow the economy or bring it to a screeching halt. Treasury bonds yielding above 9% have limited downside risk." To this the editor adds: "We're buying, too! Bond investors face record payoffs."

When Robert Acker of *The Acker Letter* highly recommended some little known companies in an article, an editor cautiously included a box: "*PF* suggests you get to know the companies recommended before committing any money. Get their latest annual and quarterly reports." He then supplied addresses and telephone numbers.

A Gloom-and-Doomer

The Holt Advisory has been a particularly gloomy letter for the past few years. It bases its investing themes upon the huge volume of private, corporate and government debt overhanging the American and Latin American economies.

If readers followed the letter's advice, they generally remained out of the market through the great bull market of 1982-1987. Articles emphasize the worth of cash. Tabulations of bank failures appear frequently. Well before the general media saw troubles in the savings and loan industry, *The Holt Advisory* warned readers of the coming financial disaster.

Some 1989 articles included: "Don't Expect the Takeover Boom to Last"; "How Corporate Earnings Will Be Hurt"; "Coming Squeeze on Banks' Profits"; and "Small Investors Continue to Shun Stocks."

The letter emphasizes the preservation of capital above everything else. It stresses the value of compound interest as an investing tool of major significance.

A Powerhouse Letter

The Outlook, Standard & Poor's conservative, fundamental, weekly newsletter, ranks as one of the oldest in the business, having been published for more than fifty years. It also has one of the highest circulations of all the letters.

Periodically, it cites industries estimated to outperform others, along with the laggards. Arnold Kaufman, the editor, explains why the industries appeal and why they don't. A list of "action" stocks names ten headed for superior price performances, according to the letter.

Subscribers receive lists of high-yield stocks and bonds, growth stocks, depressed stocks due for turn-arounds, shares with income plus inflation protection, speculative stocks and of foundation stocks for long-term holding.

A Maverick Fundamentalist

The Independent Investor is an oddity among newsletters. Though Fidelity Investments, the big brokerage-mutual fund company, owns it, the letter maintains editorial independence. The eight-page publication features articles bearing on the economy, equities purchases and on mutual fund investing (all funds, not just Fidelity's). It selects quotable items from other investment letters and offers their ideas.

Each issue contains a four-page supplement composed of technical indicators, charts, lists and a survey of market timers' letters. The data provides a quick capsule report of key factors affecting the market. The lists include top-performing mutual funds, an insider transaction report and a brokers' survey of recommended top stocks for purchase.

Fundamental letters like these represent only one part of the money media field. Other money managers and letter writers use charts, graphs and technical indicators to present their views. If you don't understand technical analysis, the language may sound as complicated as that of a computer enthusiast explaining why you must alter the CONFIG.DB file when changing d-BASE II to run "color" on your computer.

Even if your opinion of technical analysis matches that of a pure fundamentalist like Charles Allmon, you should at least listen to what technicians say. They may provide some profit-boosting ideas. The next chapter looks at some of them.

Chapter 9

Reaping Dollars With Technical Analysis

"TECHNICAL PICTURE: Neutral bordering on negative. Recent market consolidation has not led to improvement. Waning momentum and negative monetary background point to increasing risk."

Does that make any sense to you? If so, you understand technical stock market information. If not, you may need educating.

The above comment in *Bob Nurock's Advisory* shows what you encounter in a technical market letter. Don't be turned off too soon in this case, however. Nurock supports his technology with cogent interpretations for the lay person. His letter also carries a usable model portfolio for profitable stock picking assistance. Your basic goal should be to bank honest money, even if you don't exactly know how you made it. However, if you don't know what you are doing, you face high odds trying to make anything—and maybe even keeping what you already have! It pays to understand market technicians and how they operate.

THE MARKET TECHNICIAN

Like other stock technicians, Nurock studies market measuring indicators and mass psychology to determine investment actions. Statistical wizards like him analyze such things as the volume accumulation and distribution of shares, the relationship of stock prices to their moving averages and the changes of momentum and velocity for the market and for individual shares. They also study bullish or bearish sentiment and dozens of other factors.

"All that technical analysis really consists of is the study of price and volume relationships to gain an insight into future trends," says confirmed technician Stan Weinstein, editor and publisher of *The Professional Tape Reader*, a technical investing newsletter.

He makes it sound easy, as if you, too, will gain insights from charts and technical data. The uninitiated require an abundance of faith as they note technicians charting indices or marking graphs, then drawing conclusions about the future not readily apparent to everybody else.

All statistics of market activity, by definition, come from the past. Doubters of technical analysis can argue that data only tells you what *has* happened. Investors want to know what *will* happen.

Technicians' Claims

Technicians, however,insist that with the right statistical formulas they can clarify if not predict the future. Jay Schabacker, a money manager and long-time investment letter writer, says: "Conditions in the economy and their impact on various investments tend to run in cycles or patterns. If you know them, you can profit handsomely at quite moderate risk when they repeat, as they inevitably do."

If market activity repeats, as it seems to over time, then all you need do is study the statistics and indicators for patterns, or so say the technicians. Those market blueprints create the bible for their gospel.

SOME TECHNICAL ANALYSIS TENETS

The litany of market conclusions stemming from this reasoning could fill pages. Low participation of shares in market advances denotes internal weakness, so look out. A lack of breadth spells trouble. Short sellers should avoid a stock that rises above its 30-day moving average.

This may sound like gibberish to some people. But, consider again the preceding paragraph. "Low participation?" This means that only a few shares are rising in value when the Dow Jones Industrial Index shows a gain. Thirty major company stocks constitute that DJ index. Sometimes those companies account for most of the gains, while hundreds of other shares lag. So the index rises, with low participation, obviously an unhealthy sign since the market has many more losers than gainers.

"A lack of breadth" means almost the same thing as "low participation." Breadth measures the extent of share participation in the market rise. A broad market rise, obviously, is good (except for short sellers). A market that "lacks breadth" has low participation, a bad sign.

A 30-day moving average? That is the average of a market index over a month. But markets are dynamic, always moving when shares trade. Today's 30-day average may be up or down tomorrow as day 31's figure goes into the average while day 1's total is deducted for the new 30-day average. Put figures on a chart and one may see clearly what the market is doing.

An entire book could be written detailing all the tenets which comprise the lexicon of the technician. Go with the flow, meaning the flow of funds into the market, or to specific shares. This signals price rises, say technicians. Should gold shares gain, buy the metal, because a rise in stock prices usually precedes a climb in bullion quotes. When utility stocks rally following a depressed period, look for an improved broad market.

The list goes on and on.

Fundamentalists Ridicule Such Reasoning

Some fundamentalists regard technicians as witches or fortune tellers who could do better with animal entrails or crystal balls. Louis Rukeyser, the TV financial guru, featured a technical index on his program for years. It supposedly forecasted market moves. Yet his own market interpretations and his syndicated newspaper column stem from fundamental analysis. So it isn't surprising that he often smirked as he talked about that index. Moreover, he refered to its creator, the quiet, low-key Robert Nurock, as if he came from fairyland.

Forecasting the future from quotations on a stock market tape or from squiggles on a chart does seem weird to the untrained. Laymen find it easy to imagine that technicians brew statistics in a cauldron over an open fire or behind a fairy toadstool.

True Believers

Technicians see themselves differently. They regard statistics like a carpenter views tools—necessary and functional, not magical. They deny that they search for the sure-fire market predictor. They merely want something with a 9,999 to 1 probability. Technicians seldom admit that. Instead, they talk about probabilities without clarifying them. They sound like professional gamblers who only bet on what they believe is a sure thing.

"To successfully forecast the market and to profit handsomely from it, learn to play the odds," says Weinstein. He insists that "the tape tells all" you need know about the market. By that he means the ticker tape which spews a steady flow of price quotations for listed shares during trading hours.

ROOTS OF TECHNICAL ANALYSIS

Technical market analysis started long ago when traders noted how various factors affected prices. Those might have been seasonal changes, weather patterns, wars, political disturbances. As early as the 16th century, economists like Sir Thomas Gresham wrote intellectual tracts theorizing how markets behaved.

By the 19th century, a considerable volume of economic literature existed. However, in that century, insider information outweighed everything else for market speculators. You needed access to the right financial syndicate to make money. If you knew the right people, you grew rich. If not, you didn't.

The Dow Jones Index

Technical analysis owes much to Charles Dow, one of the founders of *The Wall Street Journal* and creator of the first Dow Jones Index in 1884. A refinement, the first DJ Industrial Average, appeared in 1896. That tabulation averaged share prices of twelve companies. These were:

American Cotton Oil	Laclede Gas
American Sugar	National Lead
American Tobacco	North American
Chicago Gas	Tennessee Coal & Iron
Distilling & Cattle Feeding	U.S. Leather, pfd.
General Electric	U.S. Rubber

"Dow found charts and statistics useful and in his editorials advised traders to keep various records on individual stocks as well as the full list," says William S. McSherry, the now-retired, long-time manager of news department services for *The Wall Street Journal*.

By the time that index appeared, stock markets had evolved into something approaching those of today. Investors did appreciate all possible analytical aids, but Dow did not visualize his indices as forecasting tools. He saw them as helpful statistics which showed only what had happened and was happening.

The Dow Theory

Still, Dow laid the foundation for what later became known as the Dow Theory, a veteran technical tool. Dow possessed an analytical

mind and he liked to educate as well as report. He believed
investors' sentiment moves markets, with rises or falls coming in
successive waves to a climax. Success goes to those who first recognize switches in the market's direction, he said.

That theory formed the basis for much technical analysis in the
first half of this century. Dozens of investment letters developed
around it. Interpreters filled shelves of libraries with books about it.
Among the most notable was Samuel Nelson, who published *The
ABC of Stock Speculation* in 1902, the year of Dow's death, giving
credit to the latter for much of his own analysis.

The world's Samuel Johnsons need their Boswells. William Peter
Hamilton, the *Journal's* editor in the first quarter of this century,
filled that role for Dow. He named the wave theory of markets
"The Dow Theory." Then he compressed Dow's thoughts into a
book, *The Stock Market Barometer*, which introduced the concept to a
wide audience in 1922.

The supposition contends that in a bull market, peaks on a chart
of the Dow Jones Industrial Average rise ever higher, with each
successive valley bottoming at a higher level than its predecessor.
Should the reverse occur, stock prices are declining in a bear market. If the Transportation Index adopts the same trend as the DJIA,
this "confirms" the overall market direction.

APPLYING THE DOW THEORY

Loyal adherents like Richard L. Evans, editor of *Dow Theory Forecasts*, still utilize the Dow Theory as the basic tool for market forecasting. Often they add their own refinements to the technique,
jealously guarding their proprietary data.

Richard Russell, the thin-haired, low-key editor of *Dow Theory
Letters* is another strong advocate of the Dow idea. With it, he popularized technical analysis for ordinary investors two decades ago.
Over the years, he developed his own easily understandable style
for transmitting information to the less informed.

"He is a man of great intellectual honesty," says Howard Ruff,
high praise in a field where letter writers often equivocate even
when praising friends. Many editors perch on intellectual fences so
that readers can not hold them accountable for a wrong call.

Not so with Russell. He checks his technical paraphernalia, reads their messages. Then he reports to subscribers in a straight, home-spun style. In 1984, when most economists worried about inflation, Russell declared that "we will go into deflation." Time proved him right. In 1989, he predicted the market was moving into a long-term bear market which could last for years.

ANOTHER WAVE THEORY: THE ELLIOTT WAVE

Arthur Merrill, editor of *Technical Trends*, charted every bull and bear market since 1896 to compile his databank of indices and market reactions. He rates special mention for writing a complete description of the Elliott Wave Theory, the arcane system popularized by Robert R. Prechter, Jr., in his letters, *The Elliott Wave Theorist* and *The Elliott Wave Commodity Forecast*.

R.N. Elliott developed the idea over fifty years ago, and today the forty-year old Prechter (Yale '71) ranks as his number one disciple. The theory says the stock market moves in patterns or waves determined by market momentum, prices, advance/decline ratios, time cycles and investor psychology. During a bear market, stocks move down in five waves and up in three counter-trend waves, Elliott said. Wave numbers reverse in a bull market.

The idea sounds and is complicated. Even practitioners don't always agree concerning timing of the wave stages. Many of Prechter's readers don't understand the theory, either. They accept the editor's interpretations and base market action accordingly.

Prechter, however, achieved a brilliant market timing record with it. Lately, his data shows that America heads for the worse depression since the Thirties.

The wave theory novice flounders in a sea of market combers without a guide like Prechter or fellow believers Daniel L. Ascani, editor of *The Elliott Wave Principle Forecast* or Peter Eliades, editor, *Stock Market Cycles*.

Before dismissing the theory offhand, note that cycles do occur regularly in nature, the economy, social affairs and elsewhere. Seasonal patterns exist. So do long-term weather changes such as Ice Ages. Economically, booms and recessions occurred throughout history.

MARKET INDICES AND SYSTEMS

The Dow Jones Index serves as the key index for market analysis under the Dow Theory. But investors developed numerous other indices for their toolkits as the years went by. When interpreted for buying or selling, an index or series of indices becomes a trading system.

Assemble 100 technicians in a room and you may hear of 100 different market systems. Certain techniques do possess universality. All watch for patterns like the interest rate inverted curve, the trend of the advance-decline line and the 39-day moving averages of stock prices.

The Stock Market Risk Indicator

Gray (cq) Cardiff of the *Sound Advice* letter developed this indicator. Tracing statistics for the past one hundred years, he noticed a relationship between stock and single-family home prices.

These markets compete for investment dollars. When investors buy homes, they reduce purchases of stocks, and vice versa. Cardiff traced this phenomenon historically and created a risk indicator based on the ratio of stock to house prices.

Cardiff says: "When this ratio is high, as it was just before the stock market crash of 1987, it climbs over 2.0 on my index and signals that stocks are risky. Houses are a safer investment."

Conversely, when the ratio drops below 1.0, stocks offer the best potential, he says. By following signals of the last ninety years, investors would have ridden every major bull market and avoided every crash, says Cardiff.

Moving Averages of Market Prices

Anybody using technical data soon learns that moving averages of market prices play an important role in technical analysis. As an example, *The Telephone Switch Letter* follows a 39-week moving average to generate switches into or out of mutual funds (Chapter 10).

Proponents utilize the average of the New York Stock Exchange Composite Index or of Standard & Poor's 500 Index as of the end of each of the past thirty-nine weeks. Every week, the investor computes a new average for the market, dropping the earliest weekly figure and adding the latest for the average. (Most major newspapers publish the figures).

On a chart, week-by-week figures provide an effective way to follow market trends. When the index rises above the 39-week average, this signals good times for stocks, according to technicians. Mutual fund switch investors using this system then shift into equity funds. Conversely, when the index bearishly falls below the average, investors switch into safe money funds.

First-Hour Trading Index

John Dessauer, editor of *Dessauer's Journal*, values an index of the first hour of trading on the New York Stock Exchange. It measures sentiment of European buyers, who usually deal early in the day. Often that sentiment on the other side of the Atlantic sets the pace for the rest of the day in the American market, says Dessauer.

Smart Money Flow Indicator

Somewhat similar is another indicator developed by Lynn Elgert, editor of the *Lynn Elgert Report*. He believes that steep declines in the first hour of trading followed by neutral or higher prices shows that smart money is buying. If first hour trading starts strong, then slows to neutral or decline, smart money is selling. By charting this against the Dow Jones Industrial Average, he created what he terms his "Smart Money Flow Indicator." Smart money action precedes changes on the DJIA, he says. So, using the index, an investor may forecast the market.

Relative Strength Measure

Dan Sullivan, editor of *The Chartist*, uses relative strength data to select individual stocks. Relative strength measures the performance of a particular share against that of sister shares or a market proxy such as Standard & Poor's 500 Index. If IBM, for instance, rises while other computer stocks decline, its relative strength is said to be strong, a favorable sign. With a reverse pattern, the trend may be bearish for IBM.

Nurock's Technical Market Index

You may know of this index if you watched *Wall Street Week*. You may be familiar with Nurock, too, from his many appearances as the "chief elf" on that show. Bespectacled Nurock does indeed look elfish, with his beard sprinkled with gray, small stature and mild manner. But professionals value his Technical Market Indicator (TMI) because it has been useful to them. Nurock has since left the show, taking his index with him. It has been revised and now is available only to his clients.

The index consists of sets of negative and positive economic and market indicators. Tabulate figures derived from these indicators and you produce either a negative, a positive or a neutral figure. The negatives measure the trend and strength of a forthcoming downturn, and vice versa for the positives. A neutral figure predicts no change.

Nurock, editor of *Bob Nurock's Advisory*, illustrates a point. When technicians develop a worthwhile proprietary market index or system, they may hoard the idea and try to get rich in the market with it. They also may seek wealth by launching an investment letter and selling their thinking to the public.

Nurock and many others have followed the latter path.

TECHNICAL MARKET LETTERS

Technical market letters enable you to tap the thinking of some of the best technical analysts in the country, for a price. Among them is James Dines, an investment letter veteran, who calls himself "the original gold bug." He employs a cluster of indices coupled with the experience gained through decades of market watching to write and edit his *The Dines Letter*.

Robert Kinsman's *Low Risk Growth Letter* aims to preserve the capital of his subscribers. He uses both fundamental and technical analysis to reach his conclusions. But, the manner in which he quotes his bear market indicators shows that he doesn't ignore technical indicators when they flash red.

Norman Fosback, a forty-one-year old market pro, edits five market letters from his Fort Lauderdale, Florida, headquarters. *Market Logic* and *Mutual Fund Forecaster* are the best known. He uses forty market indicators to shape advice in those letters.

Other technical letters include *Investors Intelligence, Margo's Market Monitor, McKeever Strategy Letter, Mutual Fund Strategist, The Option Advisor* and *The Professional Investor*. Each offers its own particular style of analysis.

InvesTech Market Analyst also employs technical and fundamental data for sharp market conclusions. That letter and *InvesTech Mutual Fund Advisor* are both edited by James Stack, from Montana. With help of electronic aids, he proves that investment letters can be produced in the great outdoors as well as on Wall Street.

Technical Trends *Newsletter*

Technical Trends tracks over fifty indicators and presents them to you, thus saving you considerable work should you be serious about technical analysis. The useful market aspects it follows range from relative strength to support/resistance levels and from advance/decline trends to the short interest ratio.

A Star Performer

Promotional advertisements for Martin Zweig's letters make strong claims, too, yet results support them. "ON BLACK MONDAY, THE DOW PLUNGED 22%. *THE ZWEIG FORECAST* PORTFOLIO CLIMBED 9%," proclaims a headline over an advertisement for this letter. Its model portfolio gained nearly 400 percent from 1980 to 1989, well above the rise in Standard & Poor's 500 Index in the same period.

Zweig also publishes the well-regarded *Zweig Performance Rating Report* and co-publishes *The Bond Fund Timer* with Ned Davis. The *Davis/Zweig Futures Hotline,* a telephone service, offers a market timing model which *Timer Digest* rates among the top ten timers operating on Wall Street.

A TECHNICIAN IN ACTION

Charles LaLoggia focuses upon takeover targets in his twelve-page *Special Situation Report*. Over the last few years, he showed unusual prescience in locating such corporations.

He locates prospects by searching for companies with undervalued assets and high cash flows. For market forecasting, he favors four technical monetary indicators: (1) the yield on three-month Treasury bills versus the yield on the Standard & Poor's 500 Stock Index; (2) the interest yield curve; (3) money supply growth; and (4) the Federal Reserve Discount Rate.

When the interest on three-month T bills reaches two times the yield on the S&P 500, the market generally falls, he says. For instance, if you can receive 8 percent on T bills with S&P companies paying an average dividend of 4 percent or less, look out.

The interest yield curve mentioned above represents the relationship between long-term and short-term rates. Usually long securities provide higher yields than the short. Investors expect a higher rate for the risks when their money is tied up for years than when funds are borrowed for a few months.

If short-term rates exceed the long-term rates, Wall Street says the yield curve is "inverted," or negative. That generally ushers in recessions and bear markets.

Money supply growth, the third point LaLoggia watches, involves the Federal Reserve Board's manipulation of the money supply by restricting or increasing the flow to banks.

If the money supply expands at a higher pace than the growth of the Gross National Product plus inflation, this is considered a plus for economic activity. If the supply contracts, the economy should slow over a period of time.

The fourth of LaLoggia's indicators concerns what has come to be known as the "Three Steps and a Stumble Indicator." Should the Federal Reserve Board raise its discount, that action restricts the economy. One increase doesn't worry Wall Street very much. Three in a row rings alarms. This usually leads to a stumble (a market downturn).

Statistics support the theory.

CHARTS FOR PROFITABLE ANALYSIS

Numerous services provide ready-made charts for a fee. They include Commodity Trend Service, Securities Research Co., *Daily Graphs*, M.C. Horsey & Co., Inc. and Mansfield Chart Service.

Courses in Chart Reading

Standard & Poor's *Trendline* resembles a mail order course in chart reading. It teaches the basics of various market indicators for use either with your own or with ready-made charts.

The International Institute for Technical Research publishes a five-tape video course in technical analysis. It proceeds from the basics through price patterns, support and resistance trendlines and momentum factors to mechanical trading systems. Compiled by Martin J. Pring, the package sells for $375, or as separate lessons at from $95 to $115 each.

COMPUTERS FOR TECHNICIANS

The computer opened a vast number-crunching field for technical investors. Software packages enable even novices to handle technical analysis, perhaps not with the best of the professionals, but at least well enough to pass.

Softwear Packages

Hundreds of software packages appear on the market. These do everything from monitoring your holdings to technical charting. Some are simple. The best require a modem hookup to Ma Bell or a Baby Bell, plus access to a database such as *Dow Jones/News Retrieval*.

Value Line, Inc., says more than 40,000 investors now use its software. Its *Value/Screen II* offers up to twenty criteria for selection of stocks. Pick your criteria; then your computer provides a tailor-made list of attractive share picks.

A rundown of software available for the mass market includes: Charles Schwab's *The Equalizer*; Dow Jones' *Market Analyzer Plus*;

Andrew Tobias' *Managing Your Money; Personal Financial Planner; Compustock, Telescan Edge* and several hundred more. Standard & Poor's, for instance, has *Trendline II* and *Trendline Pro* for technical investors and *Stockpak II* for fundamental investors.

New electronic software comes onto the sales market steadily. Some offer little more than a new way to balance your checkbook. Others include technical and fundamental portfolio management plus hookups with a broker for trading via computer.

Market Forecasting

"PLAY THE MARKET ON YOUR KEYBOARD" reads the headline on an ad for *The Market Forecaster*. You load it into your computer, then punch in statistics from *Barron's* into the program. You receive forecasts of various market moves, claims the promotion.

"Whether to buy stocks or mutual funds, or retreat to the sidelines? That's the question, and our unique software is the answer. It actually lets you predict the magnitude and direction of stock market movements over the next two to four months," says William Finnegan Associates, Inc., *The Market Forecaster's* creator. The tab ranges up to $295.

Databases for Technicians

If you connect to a service like *DJ/NR* or *CompuServe*, the volume of information available reaches astronomical heights. You punch commands and wade through menus that whisk you into specific stock data, markets, news stories, Securities and Exchange Commission reports and the pages of dozens of publications.

Databases include *DJ/NR, Knight-Ridder, CompuServe, Smartvest, The Source, Quotron, Prodigy, Warner Computer, ComStock,* Citicorp's services, *Telerate, Reuters* and more. *CompuServe* claimed nearly 500,000 subscribers in late 1989. *DJ/NR* had over 310,000, with Knight-Ridder neck-and-neck with the Dow Jones subsidiary. Mead Corp.'s *Lexis, Nexis* and *Medis* counted 210,000. *Prodigy* reported 125,000 clients.

Some networks focus only upon investing, others also offer additional services. So shop carefully.

Computer Trading

Fidelity Investments and discount brokerage houses lead in computer trading. Full-line brokers discourage it. They fear it negates broker-trader relationships. With computer trading, low-paid order filing clerks can replace high-paid brokers. Brokerage houses dislike transferring trade control to clerks until they're sure their businesses can dispense with brokers.

UPDATING YOUR COMPUTER TECHNOLOGY

Shop wisely if you are interested in computers. New developments arise so fast that anything written here may be outdated when you go electronic. Before buying, make certain that the packages you prefer fit your system.

For more electronic information, subscribe to personal computer magazines like *Wall Street Computer Review, PC Computing,* or *Personal Computing.* Consider also *Computerized Investing,* the bimonthly of the American Association of Individual Investors. AAII also offers a worthwhile book, *The Individual Investor's Microcomputer Guide,* on sale to AAII members for $19.95.

Books on technical analysis abound. A few to get you started: Terry Jeffers' *The Computerized Investor* (Breakthrough Publishing); Norman G. Fosback's *Stock Market Logic* (Institute for Econometric Research); Stan Weinstein's *Secrets for Profiting in Bull and Bear Markets* (Dow Jones-Irwin); Martin J. Pring's *Technical Analysis Explained* (McGraw-Hill); and Martin Zweig's *Winning on Wall Street.* Bookstores offer these and numerous others, and your library may assist, too.

Small investors usually avoid technical analysis because it takes work. Moreover, they don't invest enough to justify the cost of computer portfolio analysis. Many invest in mutual funds to avoid investing drudgery. Often, glowing promotions lured them into funds. The typical tale claims that fund money managers assume all your portfolio troubles. If you buy a good fund and stick to it, you can't lose.

It sounds wonderful. Over the last dozen years, though, mutual fund investing changed from buy-and-hold to something different. That change spawned a coterie of letters devoted solely to improving your returns from funds. Let's turn our attention now to mutual fund advisors.

Chapter 10

Profiting From Mutual Funds

MUTUAL FUND HISTORY

Mutual funds had functioned for decades without arousing much excitement among investors. Before the 1929 market crash, they generally operated as trusts. That name developed an odious reputation when many funds folded during the depression.

Promotions Proliferate and Sales Zoom

Over the last couple of decades, the industry honed its promotional talents. Funds without sales charges promoted "no-loads" as a selling tool. Brokers loved funds because they easily could bury their own high fees. Funds lowered entry minimums to bid for small investors. Wall Street developed the money fund, which operates like a secure bank account with much higher returns. Financial companies offered whole families of equity, bond or balanced funds.

Mutual fund sales soared. Twenty years ago, nine million investors held $57 billion in a few hundred funds. At start of 1990, more than thirty million held $1 trillion in 2,700 funds. The Investment Company Institute, a fund trade association, says "mutual funds, including money market funds, are owned by about a quarter of U.S. households."

UNMASKING MUTUAL FUNDS

Dick Fabian, exudes success and the self-confidence of one who knows his way around. He launched his *Telephone Switch Letter* thirteen years ago at home in Huntington Beach, California, with his thirty years in finance and investment as background. The dining room table doubled as his desk. His wife, Marie, became his "staff."

He thought that, through his letter, he could show mutual fund buyers how to earn a 20 percent annualized compounded growth rate. At that time, such investors seldom depended upon advice letters. Most wanted to avoid the hassle of putting money to work. Fund managers advertised themselves as financial specialists who offered the benefit of their vast experience. It seemed logical to investors to let them handle money without any "back-seat driving."

But Fabian knew something that most fund investors did not. Managers don't automatically handle your money with the financial acumen of Zurich bankers. Some do well; others don't. You pay a price if you trust your money to any of the latter.

"Those who bought mutual funds and put them away, following the old buy-and-hold strategy, were gravely disappointed," says Fabian. "So-called professionals, in most cases, didn't even do as well as the market averages."

FUND SWITCHING

Fabian advocated a system not generally practiced by smaller investors—fund switching. He noted that mutual fund performances differ widely. At a particular time, shares of some funds rise while others sink in value. So he reasoned that smart investors could benefit mightily by switching from a dormant fund into a mover, just as they improve holdings by selling a lemon stock to reinvest in a promising growth share. Fabian tailored his letter to explain just how readers could do that.

Says Fabian: "No matter what the political climate, there is always at least one market segment where you can make money."

Suppose a volatile market heightens the risk? In this case, instead of switching into another equity or bond fund, you would transfer your cash into a money fund. If you are a Fabian subscriber, you then wait until his letter tells you which mutual fund or funds to buy. Meanwhile, of course, your accumulation earns a return in the money fund.

The Idea Takes Hold

Fabian floated his letter at just the right time. It caught a growth wave from the 1980's stock boom, which swept the mutual fund industry with it. The *Telephone Switch Letter* thrived. Today, Fabian serves 44,000 subscribers from a modern, 18,000 square-foot office which reflects prosperity. An enlarged staff produces an investment letter, which still remains a family enterprise.

America rewards successful entrepreneurs. Fabian admits to being "a millionaire several times over," one of many such among investment letter writers.

Switching Endorsed

Fabian certainly wasn't alone in recommending fund switching. As far back as the mid-1970s, Jay Schabacker, editor of the *Mutual Fund Investing* letter, and others urged fund investors to spread risks and switch.

Schabacker, a money manager, says: "When a particular market is rising—say stocks or gold—you can place a phone call and switch more of your money into top performing funds that invest in stocks or gold—and ride the market up for handsome profits. But, when the market looks weak, you can switch your money out of stocks and into safe, secure money funds, and earn the highest rates on cash."

Some Funds Oppose Switching

Fund managers, however, complain that market timing distorts their operations. Switchers shift holdings in and out of funds as often as thirty-two times a year. Money may move in and out of funds so fast that officials scurry to invest it, then must work overtime to raise cash when timers sell.

Some firms respond by restricting switches or assessing charges for them. Fidelity, for example, charges .75 of 1% for short-term trades for its Select funds. This elicits protests from switchers, who want no restrictions at all on their market moves.

Other fund families, unhappy at watching money depart, sneak redemption fees into the fine print of contracts. Such fees vary. Some are flat charges, say 2 percent of your holdings. Others might be levied according to a declining schedule; thus, the assessment may be 5 percent if you switch within a year, 4 percent in the second year, 3 percent in the third and so on.

ADVISORY LETTERS PROLIFERATE

Today, an estimated seventy advisory letters cater to the mutual fund market. All are eager to help you. They tell you which funds to buy, which to avoid, when to switch. They distill technical data and present findings in readable articles.

They range from the *InvesTech Mutual Fund Adviser* to the *United Mutual Fund Selector*. You find the words *Mutual Fund* followed by such titles as *Advantage, Investing, Monitor, Specialist, Strategist, Values* and many more.

Mutual Fund Forecaster's *Advice*

Norman G. Fosback, editor of *Mutual Fund Forecaster*, utilizes a basket of market indicators for his conclusions. A favorite is the average dividend yield of Standard and Poor's 500 Stock Index. Says Fosback: "When the dividend yield on the 500 runs 5.5 percent or more, that's bullish; under 3 percent is bearish."

Simple! This formula is so simple that many investors pay no attention to it. Fosback analyzed market statistics back to 1926 and found that this indicator *has never been wrong when it flashed a bearish signal!* It does seem worth adding to your collection of market analysis tools.

With Fosback's letter, you need not bother to analyze funds. *Mutual Fund Forecaster* does it for you. It carries a list of forty mutual fund "Buy Recommendations" on page one of every issue.

Fosback's Fund Stars

A cluster of five funds listed as the "Best Buy Recommendations" tops that group. At start of 1989, the letter's top five were listed as below:

Risk Rating	Mutual Funds	1-Year Profit Projection	Combined Sales & Red. Fees
Very High	Quest Value Cap.	+20%	—
High	Gabelli Equity Tr.	+16%	—
Medium	Fidelity Capital Apprec.	+26%	3.0%
Low	Dreyfus Capital Value	+15%	4.7%
Very Low	Price Rowe Equity Inc.	+17%	None

(Quest Value and Gabelli Equity are closed-end funds which trade like stocks, so they have no sales or redemption fees.)

Inside the twelve-page monthly issue of *Mutual Fund Forecaster*, a tabulation of nearly 500 funds shows the profit projections and risk ratings, performances, telephone numbers and charges assessed by each.

No-Load Fund Investor's *Profit Stars*

Sheldon Jacobs edits *No-Load Fund Investor*, which notes the performances of over 500 no-load and low-load equity and bond funds, plus 120 money and 70 closed-end funds every month. He names the top 20 no-loads for the past month and year.

The July, 1989 issue, for instance, cited Fidelity Sel Broadcast/Media Fund as a top performer. Benham Target 2015 (2), Fidelity Sel Restaurant (3), Kaufmann (4) and Janus (5) followed in that order.

Three model portfolios in this letter, the "Wealth Builder," the "Pre-Retirement" and the "Retirement," provide cues for handling your investments. Still, neither these nor any other model portfolios should be set in concrete.

MARKET TIMERS

Obviously, a switch mutual fund investor must know when to move from a dud fund to a producer. You can depend upon one particular advisory letter, waiting for its directions. You also can subscribe to market-timer letters to support whatever your mutual fund guide advises. Timers seek to anticipate market swings, then advise clients to get in or out. They operate with statistics, technical charts, various market indexes and arcane formulas which may be proprietary. Some editors concentrate upon mutual funds in their evaluations, too.

One such is Paul Merriman, Seattle-based editor of *The Fund Exchange* letter. He writes a nationally syndicated mutual fund newspaper column, handles over $50 million as a money manager and lectures to investors on market timing. He heartily believes that indicators give market signals which experts can read.

"This helps you to determine when to move cash from an equity or growth investment into a money fund, or from a money market fund back into the equity or growth fund," he says.

BUYING MUTUAL FUNDS

Investigate all applicable charges before you buy any fund. For example, most of American Capital's funds have a 9.3 percent sales charge. Several Dreyfus funds don't apply any. Neither do Evergreen and a few more. If you purchase a fund through a broker, the front-end load, or sales charge, amounts to 4-9 percent or more.

With a 9 percent charge, every $1,000 delivers only $910 into the investment—the broker collects a $90 commission. That is a stiff load, indeed, for funds can lose money as well as make it. One particular fund has a 13.6 percent load, yet it lost money from August, 1987 into early 1989. Should you pay a commission to buy that?

Brokers and Funds

Despite their stiff charges, brokerage houses do play an important roll in mutual fund investing. At the start of 1989, fund assets including money funds of leading brokers in billions totaled as follows: Merrill Lynch, $65; Dean Witter, $34.5; Shearson Lehman Hutton, $33.2; Prudential-Bache, $22.7; and Goldman Sachs, $12.6 billion.

Little correlation exists between a fund's charges and its performance. The Merrill Lynch Pacific Fund has performed impressively ever since formed, while some high-cost broker funds performed miserably for the past decade.

Go For No-load Funds

Market professionals in general insist that low- or no-load funds do just as well or better than those with high sales charges. Other things being equal, it pays to select no-load funds, preferably within a fund family.

However, funds now add so many fine print charges into contracts that the term "no-load" becomes deceptive. In fact, the No-Load Mutual Fund Association, a group of eighty companies with over 525 funds, renamed itself the Mutual Fund Education Alliance. Says one official: "We intend to educate consumers so that they better understand any charges which might be involved."

Major fund families such as Benham Capital, Columbia Funds, Fidelity, Vanguard, Strong, Dreyfus and others sell their funds directly to the public with no front-end loads or with lesser fees than encountered at brokerage firms. Remember to make sure that you can switch among funds in a family before you buy in.

Deal directly with a fund if possible, rather than through an intermediary who will want a commission. Financial publications carry fund ads with toll free telephone numbers. Advisory letters, too, provide data, including telephone numbers.

An Investing Strategy

Burt Berry, editor of *No-Load Fund X*, a San Francisco-based fund letter, advises fund investors to continually rotate holdings into top performers. In a recent study, Berry found that few star funds remain hot for long. None of the top twenty-five funds of 1983 remained in that same group at the end of 1988.

He recommends buying only funds from the top five or ten among the 2,700 operating. He tells subscribers to sell any fund which slips from the top group. Then he advises transferring proceeds into new members of the top cluster.

The stars don't change positions in a group. One may fall from the leaders this month, another next month. So switching among funds need not be an emotional outburst of mass asset transfers.

Over Switching

Churning an account adds to costs. Examine all the related charges and be sure you benefit before you switch. "Much scientific evidence indicates that short-term trading does not work over the long term and the tax consequences make it even worse," says G.W. Perritt, president of Investment Information Services, Inc. of Chicago, which publishes *The Mutual Fund Letter*.

Every time you switch, you owe an accounting to the Internal Revenue Service on your next return. Moreover, keeping track of switches for your taxes can be a trying job, as well as a costly one.

MONEY FUNDS

To succeed at switching, the investor needs access to a good money fund where money may be invested when equity or income funds don't look appealing. However, not all money funds are alike. Hidden management fees may take their toll.

The money fund market embraces nearly everybody who invests at some time or other. Total deposits approximate $400 billion and the figure keeps growing. Why not? For most of 1989, money funds returned over 8 percent annually. A few well managed ones actually paid over 10 percent for a time.

Investment advisors publish letters which focus on money funds. They can help you locate the most profitable opportunities for your money.

The Money Fund King

Differences among funds provide William E. Donoghue, the money expert, with a livelihood. He publishes *Donoghue's Moneyletter* and *Donoghue's Mutual Fund Almanac*. His subscribers include fund managers, banks, insurance companies and other large-scale money managers. Indeed, the finance world regards him as the doyen of money funds.

Donoghue's Money Fund Report analyzes money movements, reports rates paid by money funds and tells readers where to deposit cash for best results. His data shows that expense ratios of money funds range from .2 of 1 percent for stars to over 1 percent for the duds. The bulk of them charge .4 to .6 of 1 percent. That 1 percent plus figure doesn't sound like much, but where large amounts are involved, it is. To get rich you must not only make money—you also must be sure you do not lose any of it.

TYPES OF FUNDS

Companies offer funds to suit almost any kind of investor. This is one reason why there are now so many market letters keeping track of them. Key categories include: International, Global (which would include America also), Income, Growth, Convertible Securities, Balanced, Capital Appreciation, Equity Only, Options, High-Grade Corporate Bonds, High-Yield Corporate (Junk) Bonds, Mortgage-backed Certificates, Treasuries, Tax-exempts and so on.

The list is almost endless. You can buy them on margin or on the installment plan. "There are as many fund types as there are Baskin-Robbins flavors," states the magazine *Changing Times.*

Fund labeling can be confusing. An industry directory calls one fund a "growth" vehicle; a magazine places it in a "specialty" category; other source terms it a "sector fund." Sometimes you must search for your fund in a strange category. Does this mean it changed direction? Not necessarily. Different publications just don't agree concerning its label. You need only to recognize the problem, shrug and go about your business.

Funds with Specific Targets

The specialization of funds centers upon buyers of units, too. Lutherans, Moslems, doctors and senior citizens, among other groups, all have entire families of funds aimed at them. The Catholic Church backs a $4 billion fund family. Scudder Stevens & Clark of Boston, Massachusetts, manages a family for the American Association of Retired Persons.

Sector Funds

Sector and specialty funds cover narrow areas such as gold, strategic investing, high technology, small companies, petroleum, metals, ethical, natural resources, medical, drugs, electronics and coins.

GUIDES TO MUTUAL FUNDS

A half dozen guides are available to help you identify funds. The Investment Company Institute offers its *Guide to Mutual Funds*, available at Box 66140, Washington, D.C., 20035-6140. A deeper look is offered in the *No-Load Mutual Funds* guide of the American Association of Individual Investors (612 N. Michigan Ave., Dept. NLG, Chicago, IL, 60611). Still another guide comes from the Mutual Fund Education Alliance. Contact them at 1900 Erie St., Suite 120, Kansas City, MO 64116. *The Complete Guide to Closed-End Funds*, available from *Closed-End Fund Digest* (see address in appendix), contains information about more than 160 such funds. It was compiled by Frank Cappiello, W. Douglas Dent and Peter W. Madlem.

A Handbook For Reference

Sheldon Jacobs of the *No-Load Fund Investor* offers the comprehensive *Handbook for No-Load Fund Investors* (Box 283, Hastings-on-Hudson, NY, 10706.) It analyzes 1,250 low- and no-load funds, and provides 530 pages of data which should make you a mutual fund expert if you digest it all. Subscribe to his letter and he will sell his book and the subscription in a single package.

Donoghue's Mutual Fund Almanac

This source contains data on more than 2,200 bond, stock and money market mutual funds, and presents their five- and ten-year records. (The Donoghue Organization, Inc., Box 6640, Dept. P, Holliston, MA, 01746.)

Mutual Fund Profiles

Standard & Poor's Corp. and Lipper cooperate in the publication of the quarterly *Mutual Fund Profiles*. Each voluminous work includes evaluations and relative performances of over 750 funds. *Profiles* notes the best and the worst performers over the year to date, over one year, five years and over ten years. Statistics cover all important aspects of fund operation. An annual subscription, consisting of four quarterly issues, is costly. A few libraries possess the *Profiles*, too.

THE MUTUAL FUND INVESTORS ASSOCIATION

Fidelity, the biggest of the fund groups, with over 100 different funds, now has an association, MFIA, devoted to making fund investing more understandable. More than 40,000 Fidelity investors are members.

"MFIA is not a part of Fidelity. We are completely independent. We provide the unbiased professional information, analysis and advice needed by Fidelity investors," says Eric M. Korben, first president of the group. He also is editor of its monthly publication, *Fidelity Insight*.

GENERAL ADVISORY LETTERS ASSIST

Like many general investment newsletters, *Personal Finance* periodically looks at mutual funds. In a report, the editor rated Blanchard Government Money Market Fund and the Vanguard Money Market Trust—Prime Portfolio as top-rated money funds. Both the Blanchard and the Vanguard money funds offer telephone switches to sister funds.

No-load fund families recommended by *Personal Finance* in early 1989 were: Scudder (160 Federal St., Boston, MA, 02110) and Vanguard (PO Box 2600, Valley Forge, PA, 19482). Fund families with specialized strength named were: Benham (1-800/472-3389) for bonds and gold; Financial Programs (1-800/525-0850) for sector funds in 9 industries; and Mutual Series (1-800/448-3863) for low volatility growth.

Personal Finance also publishes a seventy-one-page directory, *4 Steps to Mutual Fund Profits*. Call 1-800/772-9200, or write to KCI Communications, Inc., PO Box 1467, Alexandria, VA, 22314-9819.

The Financial Publications

Several financial publications provide comprehensive lists and evaluations of mutual funds. Among them: *Financial World, Money* magazine, *Business Week, Investor's Daily, Personal Investing News, Changing Times* and *Forbes*. *The Wall Street Journal* periodically reports developments. Every quarter, *Barron's*, with cooperation of Lipper Analytical, publishes the performance records of funds, together with in-depth articles.

A FINAL WORD

Mutual funds traditionally overstated their returns in promotions until the Securities and Exchange Commission established new rules for reporting them. This brought some order into the situation. However, funds still like to report gains as if all investors reinvested all dividends, which they do not. Fund advertising and promotion still ring with an optimism which may exaggerate performance fact.

Don't be discouraged. Smart investors know not only how to evaluate mutual fund letters but other money letters, too. The investment newsletter industry even has its "Ralph Nader" to help you in the selection process. This gentleman doesn't please everybody in the business, but you may benefit from learning more about him in the next chapter.

Chapter 11

Evaluating Investment Letters

In 1988, prior to the November presidential election, Howard Ruff, the articulate editor of *The Ruff Times*, predicted that Michael Dukakis would win the White House. He may have been embarrassed after the election, but he did not show it.

Skilled investment advisors know that everybody makes mistakes. They also realize people forget more easily than they remember. So, whether talking politics or money, the experts often predict, hoping their hits far outnumber their misses.

THE INVESTMENT LETTER WATCHDOG

There is one individual, however, who does not forget. Mark Hulbert, the self-appointed warden of money advisors, makes a good living (and some enemies) policing investment letters. He studies 120 of the most important letters, notes predictions about market swings, stocks and other investments. With benefit of hindsight, he compares statements with actual happenings.

He wants answers to these questions: Would letter subscribers have made money by following a letter's advice? And how does a letter compare with others in its particular field? Such queries strike at the very heart of an investment letters' reason for existence.

Thus, money advisors bitterly resent them when hindsight reveals some bad calls.

You, too, want answers to the same questions, of course. With hundreds of investment letters available, selecting one or more for your investing becomes a difficult task. You need all the help you can muster. Hulbert solidifies the answers to these questions in a monthly letter, *The Hulbert Financial Digest*. Over 75,000 readers have subscribed to it and it ranks as the financial industry's most widely read letter about the performances of investment letters.

USING HULBERT'S DATA

Does this mean that investors should concentrate on letters apparently recommended by Hulbert, ignoring the others? Not necessarily. He really does not make recommendations. He objectively reports findings concerning a letter's performance. You can draw your own conclusions.

You may argue with his methodology—letter editors with low Hulbert performance ratings certainly do! They complain that he enters only buy and sell recommendations into his computer data, terming every "hold" as a sell. If the "hold" share subsequently soars in the market, that rise would not show in the letter's performance. Thus, you could overlook a letter with a stronger record than that revealed by Hulbert.

Letter editors, too, say the Hulbert system allows no room for gradations in recommendations. Editors may strongly recommendation one share, and praise another weakly. Sometimes they name shares as "speculative buys" while adding "not for conservative investors." So how, ask Hulbert's critics, can an evaluator differentiate between various shades of meaning in a letter? Computers can't do this, of course. Despite the glowing claims about the "intelligence" of computers, they face difficulties when translating subjective data into objective conclusions. A computer knows only black and white—it recognizes no shades of gray. Everything must be up or down, yes or no, plus or minus.

Unfortunately, some editors add to these difficulties by equivocating in their copy. They hedge recommendations. They may have much to say, but they don't express it positively. So Hulbert can claim that editors would have few complaints about the rating system if, in their letters, they boldly stated recommendations in the yes or no language of computers.

Hulbert remains low-key. He does not welcome clashes with letter writers. He admits the problem of dealing with ambiguous statements. Then, he methodically follows an evaluation system developed over a decade of studying letters.

He says: "There is no one correct way to deal with ambiguities, and therefore you shouldn't assume the *Hulbert Financial Digest's* resolution of them is the only way that could be chosen by fair and reasonable people."

If you like a particular letter, stick with it even if you do not see it on any of Hulbert's tabulations of top performers. Listen to what Hulbert has to say, though, when searching among little known letters for one or more to fit your portfolio. Look upon his material, coupled with the sampling described later, as aids in your selection process.

A letter which costs you a few hundred dollars a year is a bargain if you earn profits with it. In the final analysis, the investment letter for you is one which helps you make money.

HULBERT INTRODUCES ACCOUNTABILITY

Hulbert's letter does keep investment letter writers on their toes. "To say that Mark Hulbert created a revolution in the letter writing business is putting it mildly," says one money advisor. "Until he came along there was no accountability."

That is only partially true. Halfhearted attempts were made, previously, to analyze the worth of letters. None handled the job with the detachment and computer expertise displayed by Hulbert. None caught the attention of the investing public as Hulbert did.

Hulbert came upon his job as the guru of investment letters almost by chance when attending a money seminar in New Orleans. He came not as a participant, but as a political lobbyist with a message to sell to a presidential candidate.

In November, 1979, Hulbert, then twenty-four, a Kansan fresh from Oxford University with a philosophy degree, possessed the idealism and some of the iconoclasm of youth. He came to New Orleans accompanied by James Davidson, a fellow Oxford graduate, who headed the National Taxpayers' Union (NTU). NTU supported a constitutional amendment to compel balanced federal budgets. The two aimed to sell that idea to the California politician and speaker at the conference, ex-governor Jerry Brown.

James U. Blanchard III and his National Committee for Monetary Reform promoted the seminar. It attracted 5,000 investors and money advisors, including scores of investment letter writers. Some came as scheduled speakers; others exhibited their wares in the related money trade show.

The Blanchard annual seminar, launched a few years earlier, had become an institution for trading money ideas between investors and personal finance advisors. Hulbert and Davidson could not have found a friendlier place. Hard-asset fans predominated in the throng and they endorsed anything which would hamstring government spenders in Washington.

Jerry Brown, a maverick liberal, did not belong in the crowd, but presidential hopes make strange bedfellows. In 1979, Jerry Brown saw himself as a Democratic presidential candidate. Few others did then, or in 1980, either, when the race heated. It did appear, though, that the balanced budget idea might generate political ammunition for his sputtering campaign.

In a briefing, Brown listened courteously to the NTU theme. Hulbert and Davidson left convinced of a job well done. They had nothing else to do except roam the crowded halls of the Rivergate Conference Center and meet investment letter writers.

The widely varying advice of these money advisors intrigued them. They noted the hyperbole of promotional pieces for letters, the promises of wealth, the different market predictions,the conflicting recommendations. And they discovered that, despite the many publications represented in the hall, none used hindsight to tell the public how all that money advice compared with subsequent developments. Most investors had no way of checking a letter's record except by making or losing money through its recommendations. In effect, the letter industry needed a consumer champion, a personal finance Ralph Nader—or so it seemed to the two tax apostles.

Such discoveries kindled an idea: why not establish a service to evaluate investment letters and their advice? With hindsight, revealing results could be published. Investors would have their champion.

The Hulbert Financial Digest

Thus was born the *Hulbert Financial Digest*, the organ which Hulbert employs to publish his evaluations of specific investment advisory letters. Davidson helped finance the idea. Hulbert developed it. And the investment letter writing industry has never been the same since.

Barron's, the Dow Jones weekly, publicized some of the *Digest's* findings early in its existence. That fired broad interest in the budding new letter. Circulation climbed. Scores of newspapers and magazines welcomed the *Digest's* news releases.

Like many of the investment advisory editors he follows, Hulbert, too, has become a celebrity on the advisory seminar circuit. He edits his publication, speaks on platforms around the country and writes a weekly column for *Forbes*—about investment letters, naturally.

His years of investigating investment advisors has now produced a sizeable computer database on their letters, methods of operation and recommendation histories.

His book, *The Hulbert Guide to Financial Newsletters* (obtainable in many book stores), is in its third edition. It serves as a good introduction to the field of investment letters and what they do for subscribers.

TOP PERFORMING LETTERS

Based on evaluations of newsletter recommendations, the top ten performing letters in 1988, according to Hulbert's computer analysis, were:

Newsletter1988 Gain

1. *The McKeever Strategy Letter*	+133.4%
2. *Futures Hotline* (Average)	+ 60.0%
3. *Prudent Speculator*	+ 49.2%
4. *BI Research*	+ 38.7%
5. *Market Mania* (Average)	+ 35.7%
6. *The Insiders*	+ 34.5%
7. *Special Situations Report* (Average)	+ 32.2%
8. *MPT Review* (Average)	+ 29.8%
9. *Investment Reporter* (Average)	+ 28.3%
10. *Dessauer's Journal*	+ 27.7%
Wilshire 5000 Index	+ 19.7%

The gain column represents what an investor might have made had recommendations been followed religiously, with no money removed from accounts, according to Hulbert's methodology.

Consistency Counts

One year's record means little in money markets. Often, this year's heroes become next year's outcasts, and vice versa. This holds for money managers, mutual funds, investment letters or individual investors. Consistency over a period of years counts for far more than does skyrocketing for 365 days.

LONG-TERM STAR LETTERS

Hulbert now has data for enough years to show long-term as well as current performances of numerous letters. In the period from June 30, 1980 to June 30, 1988, for instance, the ten top performing market letters, according to Hulbert, were:

Newsletter	Gain
1. *Zweig Forecast*	+395.1%
2. *Value Line Investment Survey*	+348.3%
3. *The Prudent Speculator*	+311.5%
4. *Growth Stock Outlook*	+280.3%
5. *Telephone Switch Newsletter*	+236.8%
6. *Market Logic*	+227.7%
7. *The Chartist*	+220.5%
8. *Value Line OTC Spec. Sit. Service*	+204.3%
9. *Growth Fund Guide*	+197.0%
10. *No-Load Fund X*	+194.7%

Hulbert's system penalizes any letters of recent origin, for he doesn't even bother with a letter with a history under eighteen months. Moreover, Hulbert skips some of the old-timers because comments in letters cannot be fitted into his methodology. Still, he makes no claim to infallibility.

SELECTING AN INVESTMENT LETTER

"Obviously, while proven performance is the single most important factor to consider when selecting an investment advisor, other considerations must be taken into account," says Hulbert.

Ask yourself some questions before selecting an investment letter to improve your profit picture. Publishers offer so many that choosing wisely requires study. Do you invest in equities, in bonds, in options, in real estate, mutual funds or in all of these fields? Letters exist for each of these segments.

A Vast Variety Of Letters

Many letters may not match your temperament and strategies. If you don't invest in futures, you won't appreciate the *Futures Hotline*. If you hesitate, through caution, to play the takeover game, you won't enjoy Charles LaLoggia's *Special Situation Report*. Al Frank of the *Prudent Speculator* likes to use margin in his trading. Do you?

The *Defaulted Bonds Newsletter* provides current information on over 100 corporate and municipal bonds in bankruptcy or payment default. Knowledgeable investors make a lot of money with such information, but at great risk. Is that what you want?

If you believe it pays to follow investors such as Warren Buffett, the Bass brothers, David Murdock, Carl Icahn or other prominent investors, then you might like *Wealth Monitors,* which tracks what these investors do with their money.

The clarity of a letter matters, too. Advice which you can't comprehend means little unless you blindly follow somebody else's direction. Again, remember, don't invest in anything you do not understand. A blind follower is likely to become a victim.

Suitability is another factor. If you dislike technical analysis, you gain little from a chart-filled publication tailored for followers of market indicators. If you invest in mutual funds, you won't want a letter which focuses upon options trading.

SAMPLE LETTERS HELP

Once you decide upon the types of letters appropriate for your investing goals, look for samples. Many letters will send a free copy to a potential subscriber. In recent advertisements, *Grant's Interest Rate Observer* included a form for requesting a free sample. Dick Davis includes a copy of his twelve-page *Dick Davis Digest* in some of his direct mail promotions.

Samples For A Small Price

Some letter writers offer samples at a price. One dollar and a stamped return envelope brings you a copy of *Your Window Into The Future* letter. *Harry Browne's Special Reports* charges $5 each for its samples.

It only costs a postage stamp to write a courteous note to a letter inquiring about sample charges, if any. As a minimum, you will receive promotional literature for that particular letter.

Look for addresses of numerous letters in the appendix of this book. Letters advertise in financial publications like *Barron's*. Their direct mail brochures flow regularly into mailboxes.

Select Information Exchange's Samples

SIE, the country's largest financial subscription agency, sells trial subscriptions of one to five issues for over 200 investment letters. In 1989, you could sample the whole lot for $65.

At that time, the Exchange offered sample letters in specific investment areas at from $7.50 to $18 per package. That package allowed you to pick samples of 15 different letters from a selection of 33.

Groups of letters cover general investing, mutual funds, options, commodity trading, foreign investing, growth stocks, technical services, fundamental services, gold, oil, low-priced stocks and market timing. One group consists of the 20 best performing letters of the 200 plus. The Exchange's ads appear in financial magazines and newspapers. (See Select's address in appendix and write for a list of their packages.)

HULBERT'S RIVALS

Hulbert's success spawned a few rivals who have carved niches for themselves as letter evaluators. *Timer Digest* checks on the performances of the technical letters which predict swings in the stock market. Every year it names a "Timer of the Year," and the top ten in this area. *Commodity Traders Consumer Report* rates advisors in commodities according to the estimated payoffs from recommendations.

Rating The Stock Selectors lives up to its title, with reports about letters which deliver worthwhile information to subscribers. *Hard Money Digest* each year announces its "Newsletter Award of Excellence" to a top-performing investment letter. *Investment Hotline Monitor* rates the performance records of the hotlines maintained by numerous investment letters. (Select Information has that "20 best" letter package in one of its sample collections.)

None of these evaluators approach Hulbert's pre-eminence in the field of investment letters.

TRIAL SUBSCRIPTIONS

Recently, concerned with falling subscriptions, more letters have begun to offer trial subscriptions at reduced prices. A spot check of 100 letters shows that half of them now do so.

The Holt Advisory offers a cut-rate three-month trial subscription. *No-Load Fund Investor* offers a like trial at half the regular rate. Other special subscriptions trials run from one to five months at considerably reduced rates.

Value Line Survey offers a bargain ten-week trial service. If you continue with the full year, the firm credits the trial fee to your annual bill.

Standard & Poor's low-priced eight-week trial for *Trendline* amounts to a mail order introductory course in technical analysis. You receive over 3,000 individual stock charts in the deal. Says the company: "Once you learn the basics of this important tool, you probably will want to continue with the *Trendline* service."

Who might benefit from such a trial? Standard & Poor's answers: "If you maintain a stock portfolio, trade or invest, this course will give you the background material necessary to employ charts in your investment strategy."

The firm offers a cheap three-month trial for its *Outlook* letter. The deal includes an Over-The-Counter Stocks handbook, a 268-page stock guide, a 240-page bond guide and a report of emerging and special situations stocks.

Other publications offer bonuses of various types as they, too, woo subscribers. These may consist of a list of supposedly hot stocks which will make you rich. The gift might be a copy of the latest book written by the letter's producer. Stan Weinstein, editor of *The Professional Tape Reader*, throws in a copy of his book *Secrets for Profiting in Bull and Bear Markets* in his subscription deals. Mark Skousen, editor of *Forecasts & Strategies*, promises a free bonus report, "My 45 Best Investment Tips." Moreover, he discounts the price of his letter for new subscribers.

The cost of subscriptions to some of these letters is small compared to the profit potential if a few recommendations pay off, unless you invest small sums only. In that case, you shouldn't subscribe to any letter. Depend upon your local library for information as you save for more sizeable investments. (You won't make money in stocks unless you deal in 100-share lots; the odd lot trader—less than 100 shares at a time—pays too much in brokerage commissions to profit easily.)

Age Of Letters Counts

One other remark: consider the age of a letter, too, when you evaluate it for possible subscription. The *United & Babson Investment Report* began publication as the *United Business & Investment Report* in 1919. James Dines, Harry Schultz, Richard Russell, Charles Allmon and a handful of others were publishing advisory letters when younger practitioners of this art were attending kindergarten. These old-timers must have something of worth to say to investors to last that long.

When shopping for letters, your best bet is a big investment seminar. Scores of letter writers appear at James U. Blanchard III's huge investment conference held every fall in New Orleans. They set up shop at stalls, distribute free samples, answer your questions. And this is only one of the seminars where you face an avalanche of material and speeches about making money through investing.

It may be time to look at some of these affairs and their worth to you.

Chapter 12

Investment Seminars

On October 22, 1987, three days after the Black Monday stock market crash, the Russell [Kansas] Daily News carried a notice with considerable information between the lines. It read: "The GET RICH AND STAY RICH SEMINAR sponsored by First of Kansas Banking and Savings scheduled for October 24 has been cancelled until later notice." Numerous other stock market investors around the country, also, had their GET RICH AND STAY RICH plans cancelled the week of the crash.

That says much about the status of investors at that time. However, it says little about the investing seminar business itself. Around the country, money conferences, big and small, continued to attract audiences. Today, they provide another important informational platform for investors.

After the Crash, it took some time for the paralysis to dissipate. Then investors looked around and realized that they still wanted to get rich and stay rich—though not necessarily in Russell, Kansas.

SMORGASBORD OF SEMINARS

Seminar sponsors promise to help you invest your money, to teach you profitable strategies, to warn you of financial pitfalls, to slash taxes on your profits, to explain how to open a secret overseas bank account where your money has "total privacy."

Are you interested in opening a bank account in the Bahamas or the Cook Islands, or Montserrat, or Nauru? Or perhaps you would prefer to have one in the Turks and Caicos Islands, or in Vanuatu or the Mariana Islands? A pair of two-day seminars organized by WFI Corp., Beverly Hills, California, piloted investors through those and other options. One affair was held at the Hilton in New York City; the other at the Beverly Hills Hilton.

Ideal Locations

Such events might be scheduled in any part of the country, or in a foreign land—invariably in an attractive resort. Major seminar promoters prefer Florida, California, Hawaii, the Caribbean, Bermuda or the Bahamas in winter. Come summer, plush American resorts compete for this business with Alaskan cruise ships and hotels in Monte Carlo, Switzerland or other locales with good weather, great scenery and deluxe hotels. You need to search hard to find a better January location than Fort Lauderdale, Florida, the "Venice of America."

Direct mail advertising alerts you to these seminars. Some promoters of seminars offer free phone numbers to those seeking information about programs.

SOME TYPICAL SEMINARS

Generally, the investment seminar aims at conducting enough investing workshops to cover a broad array of topics. These could involve anything from mutual fund purchases to investing in tax-free bonds, and from selecting profitable stocks to portfolio diversification. They also could include all of these topics plus many more.

Charles and Kim Githler's Investment Seminars Inc. (ISI), promised that attendants at a one-day affair in San Francisco could take home numerous investment tools. These consisted of dozens of current advisory letters, annual reports and prospectuses of companies, analysis readouts of portfolios and investing books at "deeply discounted prices."

The meeting brought together some of the investing world's most prominent people as speakers. Investors not only heard them, but each went home with a workbook covering eight hours of the sessions for home study.

The speakers and workshop moderators included Charles Allmon of *Growth Stock Outlook,* Stan Weinstein of *The Professional Tape Reader,* Jay Schabacker of *Mutual Fund Investing,* Mark Hulbert of *The Hulbert Financial Digest,* Al Frank of *The Prudent Speculator,* Norman Fosback of *Mutual Fund Forecaster* and eight other editors or money managers.

At such affairs, you meet people like that and learn their investing strategies. Many of these money advisors appear at a dozen or more seminars in the course of a year.

You also may meet famous financial television personalities at some seminars. "Join Investment Seminars for an evening with your favorite host from "Wall Street Week," Louis Rukeyser," said one promotion for a five-day meeting in Fort Lauderdale in the dead of winter. If you prefer Paul Kangas, the stock market commentator on Public Broadcasting's "The Nightly Business Report," the bespectacled commentator also appeared at that particular seminar, ready to shake your hand if you encountered him.

BLANCHARD'S ANNUAL EVENT

Of course, you seek something more from these affairs than rubbing elbows with TV notables or cruising on some of the 165 miles of navigable waters within a place like Fort Lauderdale. You want to know how to make money in the market. Consider the publicity for one of James U. Blanchard's annual fall investment conference in New Orleans, biggest in the business: "Sixty five of the world's top financial experts will help you plan strategies for successful investing," promised the message. Rukeyser and Kangas both appeared at sessions, along with just about every investment letter writer of note. Henry Kissinger topped the long list of speakers. He presented his ideas about world affairs (which he understands better than most), along with possible repercussions on markets (about which he knows little).

Can you obtain enough information at these sessions to make them worthwhile? Perhaps. Most of the nearly 2,000 attendees at the last Blanchard meet seemed to think so.

That does not necessarily hold true at all seminars. They vary so widely that nobody can make a blanket endorsement or condemnation. Certain money managers make excellent teachers; others do not. A few seminar promoters understand showmanship; some do not. A handful aim at giving you your money's worth; others seek only to lighten your pocketbook.

Top seminars gather formidable rosters of speakers, and Blanchard's annual conclave in New Orleans stands high in that regard. At his 1990 conference, scheduled speakers include Charles Allmon, Richard Russell, Richard Band, Harry Browne, Adrian Day, Richard Young, Jerry Pogue, John Dessauer, Andre Sharon, Donald Rowe, William E. Donoghue and many more.

Of course, when you come right down to it, Henry Kissinger, a speaker at an earlier affair, can't tell you much that benefits your investment portfolio. But the ex-statesman does prompt you to think. That goes for another speaker there, too, who drew a big crowd—Lieutenant Colonel Oliver North.

If you attend such an affair *only* for profitable money ideas, at the Blanchard 1990 seminar you need only read notices on bulletin boards or in your workbook to locate the right conference rooms.

Experts Share Their Secrets

In one, Charles Allmon shares his latest list of super growth stocks for adding to portfolios. At another, Stan Weinstein tells how to use technical indicators. Jay Schabacker explains his market forecasting tools and their current readings. Douglas Casey warns optimist to think again.

So you want something more dramatic? How about a session with James McKeever as he explains "a tested strategy for turning $50,000 into a million dollars?" You don't have $50,000? Then, Richard Band helps with a presentation explaining how you can buy low and sell high.

At such seminars, investment advisors throw money ideas of all kinds in your direction. You catch them and add whatever seems appropriate to your investing strategies. If you attend hoping to get rich, you'll probably be disappointed. If you come to learn, you can.

INVESTMENT SHOPPING CENTERS

Major conferences sometimes host exhibitions as well as speaking and workshop sessions. The Blanchard "Investor's Market" at one of his conferences fills a cavernous New Orleans hall with brightly lit exhibit stands. Investment letter writers occupy many of the booths when not on speaking platforms. They dispense samples of their letters, explain market philosophies, answer questions and sell subscriptions.

Blanchard claims his affair "has always been the largest gathering of investment, financial, collectible exhibitors in the world." A stroll through crowded lanes among the 150 booths shows this to be a huge gathering indeed.

A Coin Market

A prominent coin dealer displays a collection of rare gold coins, brightly polished in their transparent wrappers. Tenderly, he takes a Spanish Eight Reales coin from a display case, extends it in his palm. In awed tones, he talks about the fabled Piece of Eight, first milled in 1732 at Mexico's mint, the Casa de Moneda.

Collectibles On Sale

Antique books lay on another counter, protected by a transparent sheet. The dealer dispenses brochures describing his collection. Elsewhere, stamp compilations catch attention. A booth features the autographs of important people, with George Washington's signature the showpiece.

Mel Fisher's Treasure Trove

At another of Blanchard's conferences, Mel Fisher, the dean of America's treasure hunters, displayed a staggering collection of gold artifacts from a sunken Spanish galleon. The ship went down off Key West, Florida, in 1622, and became a goal for treasure seekers for centuries. Its cargo holds contained gold bullion and artifacts worth $70 million in metal alone, worth much more as relics of another age.

Fisher located the wreck and its cargo. One of his relics on display attracted much attention: a gleaming, 15-foot gold chain weighing five pounds. Visiting women posed for photographs with the chain around their necks. It reached all the way to the carpet of the Hyatt Regency suite.

Every investor able to do so should visit at least one major seminar like Blanchard's, especially one with an attached exhibition. Such a meet provides new insights into the world of investing and the money advisors who play an important role in it.

It costs well over $1 million to host each of Blanchard's New Orleans conclaves. Major conclaves feature banquets, sightseeing trips, fashion shows and other entertainment along with investment work sessions. This most certainly holds true for any gathering in New Orleans. Blanchard hosts his seminars only a few blocks north of the filigreed balconies, the delicious aromas of Galatoire's Restaurant and other attractions which make the city's French Quarter a Creole Disneyland.

If you like pleasant weather and have the time and money for it, a seminar provides all the excuses you need for a trip. Many participants bring spouses along, though singles will find plenty of interest also.

Exhibitors host never-ending parties in hotel suites. They present small gifts like pens, cigarette lighters, ash trays, plastic shopping bags and chances to win more substantial door prizes.

People thrust copies of advisory letters, investing brochures, books and promotional literature into your hands. Everybody lugs one of more of those bags to tote away the loot.

In addition to his New Orleans conference, Blanchard hosted two other seminars in San Jose, Costa Rica and in game parks of Kenya in 1988. To keep abreast of his seminars, call 1-800/877-7633.

PROMOTERS OF MAJOR SEMINARS

Promoters of major seminars include Seminars International Inc., World Perspective Communications (1-800/333-5697), Howard Ruff National Convention, Blanchard's Investment Seminars and International Investment Seminars.

COSTS OF SEMINARS

Investors' extravaganzas like those of Blanchard or ISI welcome anybody with the seminar fee. This usually ranges from $200 to $800, plus hotel bills for three days.

A $5,000 Ticket Seminar

One 1989 seminar, held in Boca Raton, Florida, had a $5,000 per person price tag for forty people, not including the hotel bill. Participants were told to expect a 50 percent yearly return on their portfolios from information gathered at this particular affair. Such exaggerated costs—and claims—should awaken caution—if not skepticism.

Transport And Hotel Costs

Airline fares may become significant if you reside far from a scheduled seminar. Promoters, however, do obtain substantial discounts for you from regular air and hotel tariffs. Moreover, the Internal Revenue Service recognizes legitimate investing seminar expenses as deductible beyond 2 percent of adjusted income.

TYPES OF SEMINARS

Basically, seminars fall into four categories, with some overlap. These are:

1. Major, broad investing seminars, like those of Blanchard.
2. Trading system or narrow focus seminars.
3. Local seminars presented by brokers, banks, savings and loans, and other institutions.
4. Educational money seminars.

THE MAJOR SEMINAR

Major seminars usually cover three days. Speakers number from a dozen to over sixty. A half dozen big investing seminars attracted up to 5,000 each at conclaves during the stock boom days prior to October, 1987. Now, promoters cheer if an affair draws 2,000.

A Ruff Convention

Howard Ruff's seminars certainly rank among the leaders. The 57-year old money advisor conducts two every year, one in Florida, another in California. A 1989 affair in Anaheim, California, attracted 1,700, most of them subscribers to *Ruff Times*.

Over the years of Ruff's conventions, his letter's circulation has ranged as high as 100,000 plus. This provided a big market from which to draw audiences. Once, at one of these seminars, Ruff bragged to journalists that: "My subscribers range from little old ladies on Social Security to Nelson Bunker Hunt." Hunt, of course, is the one-time multi-billionaire who lost a few billion dollars trying to corner the silver market. That had nothing to do with Ruff or his advice.

An Investment Workshop And A Carnival

Ruff's subscribers don't *all* gather at his conventions; it only seems like they do. The affairs are a combination of a Reunion Day Party

in the old hometown and a carnival in Kansas plus a money conference. Some participants have attended so many of the Ruff seminars that they know everybody else. They come to meet old friends
as well as to collect profitable ideas from money managers and investing letter writers on podiums.

Ruff treats his subscribers as family. He and his wife, Kay, greet
participants in hotel lobbies or at cocktail parties. Somebody will
ask about Ruff's thirteen children and seventeen grandchildren, and
Ruff may have photographs to show.

It is not all socializing, though. Over three and a half days, the
seminar covers the dangers of inflation plus nearly every type of
investment. You hear about gold mining stocks, gold bullion and
coins, option and commodities trading, mutual funds, collectibles,
growth stocks, bonds, tax-deferred instruments, real estate, fran-
chising and entrepreneurship. At the 1988 San Francisco seminar,
over fifty exhibitors jammed the seminar's companion exhibit hall.

NARROW FOCUS SEMINAR

Narrow focus seminars spotlight a thin segment of the investing
market for a national audience. The larger ones become extravaganzas much like the major conclaves described earlier, except for the
focus.

They include the Technical Analysis Group seminar and the Futures Symposium, which feature the technical side of investing. The
Gold Show, sponsored in major American cities by Britain's *Mining
Journal,* attracts everybody of importance in gold along with numerous gold bugs who desire inside information about their favorite
metal.

The Predator's Ball

Drexel Burnham Lambert's defunct annual Predator's Ball in Beverly Hills, California, certainly ranked as a major seminar, with
3,000 in attendance at the 1989 junk bond affair. But, it wasn't open
to the general public. The conclave attracted people who borrowed
tens or hundreds of millions through junk bonds, financiers who

created and packaged them and institutional money managers who purchased them.

LOCAL SEMINARS

Local seminars, sponsored by financial planners, banks, brokers and savings and loan institutions, far outnumber all other kinds of seminars. They aim to attract new or more active customers. One or two speakers participate in what usually are two- or three-hour sessions on a couple investment topics. Usually, they cost only the wear and tear on your automobile plus gasoline to get there. When food is offered, attendants may pay a moderate fee to discourage freeloading.

A Broker Bids For Business

Typical were a series of local seminars conducted around the country by Merrill Lynch at its offices. The first, "Investment Strategies for the Bush Era," featured discussions via video by Senator Robert Dole, Congressman Daniel Rostenkowski and columnists George Will and Patrick Buchanan. At each office, Merrill Lynch brokers explained investment strategies to invited guests.

At affairs like this, be prepared for sales pitches. If you possess little sales resistance, stay away from them. If you seek more information, you might obtain it. These conclaves provide opportunities for questions which brokers or other money people dislike during trading hours. In the more relaxed, evening atmosphere, your questions receive closer attention.

Salesmanship At Sea

Brokers occasionally go far for clients. Shearson Lehman Hutton once conducted a five-day money seminar on the Queen Elizabeth 2 headed from New York to Southampton, England. Participants returned on the Concorde. American Pacific Securities held a similar series on the same ship on a 36-day Pacific cruise.

AAII SEMINARS

The American Association of Individual Investors (AAII) conducts no-frills investing workshops throughout the year for interested members. It climaxes the year with an annual National Meeting and Investment Education Seminar.

Profile of Participants

Don't disdain these affairs as being beneath you. The average AAII member earns $115,000 a year and has a $680,000 investment portfolio, not including home equity. Of the 100,000 members, 84 percent possess at least a college undergraduate degree. In 1987, a disaster year for many investors, Standard & Poor's Index noted a 2.2 percent gain. A membership survey showed AAII members averaged a return of 11 percent with their investments.

Scope of AAII Workshops

In 1989, AAII conducted sixty-five one-day seminars around the country. The spring schedule alone included affairs in Minneapolis, Detroit, San Francisco (four), Boston (four), Chicago (two), New York (two), Washington (two), Columbus, Cincinnati, Portland, Pittsburgh, Houston, Los Angeles, Kansas City, Seattle, Denver and Dallas.

Each focused upon a particular aspect of investing. These were: economic analysis; real estate investment; mutual funds; the fundamentals of investing; financial planning for households; and stock analysis and portfolio management.

Speakers came from universities, the AAII staff and from ranks of professional consultants. Attendance typically totaled about forty at each local seminar.

Fees included luncheon and refreshments at meeting breaks plus course materials. What you receive from sessions depends upon what you put into them. AAII believes that to make money, investors must work at it. Workshops involve college level, no-nonsense courses geared to make participants think for themselves. You don't attend these to get rich in one or two easy lessons.

In addition, AAII's forty-three chapters hold monthly meetings where members trade ideas and listen to money experts.

THE SCAM SEMINAR

Be careful of the local evening or one-day seminars which charge around $200 or more per person. Many are scams. Smooth operators promise in advertising to reveal profitable investing secrets, for instance, how to get rich in real estate by buying properties for nothing down.

The ads attract several hundred people, most eager to get rich, quickly. For less than $5,000 in costs, the promoters earn $40,000 to $50,000. Split three or four ways, this produces a nice one-day take. You listen to empty talks, and depart feeling ripped off.

INVESTMENT CLUBS

AAII faces competition from the 7,000 investment clubs of the non-profit, 140,000-member National Association of Investors Corp. With membership comes an *Investors Manual*, which describes how to establish and operate a club.

Better Investing serves as the group's "trade journal." It provides company profiles and a model portfolio to assist members in their investing. It also discusses strategies and shows readers how to invest for the long term.

How Clubs Operate

Each club collects a money pool for group investing as if it were a mutual fund. A typical club has ten to twenty people, meets monthly and requires monthly savings of $20 to $40 from each member. This goes into the pool for purchasing stocks, bonds or whatever appeals to the group. Members own pieces of the pot according to their contributions to it.

The average club portfolio contains about fifteen stocks worth $60,000 in total. Members research potential investments and learn sources for financial information by trading ideas at meetings. They discuss appropriate buys, sometimes argue heatedly, then select investments by vote.

Investment clubs fall into a group difficult to categorize and easily overlooked when examining the money media. Club meetings cannot be called seminars, yet they do provide somewhat the same function for the individual investor. They enable members to acquire worthwhile investing experience without risking a lot of money.

Don't overlook another part of the money media, either, as you seek information to improve your financial status. Few people realize that the United States government, too, operates a giant publishing and news network in its various departments, bureaus, commissions and agencies. Moreover, some of these entities focus upon economic, business and financial developments which directly affect your investments. The next chapter examines that situation.

Chapter 13

Profiting From Government Data

Will Rogers, the legendary humorist, liked to say: "I don't make jokes. I just watch the government and report the facts." The remark always produced a laugh. Today, investors watch Washington, too, but not for laughs.

A MONEY MEDIA GIANT

You can glean profitable ideas from bureaucrats and lawmakers if you know where to look and how to apply the knowledge. The government publishes enough newspapers, magazines, press handouts, brochures and other printed matter to form an industry by itself. True, not all deal with financial and money topics, but many do and that is why investors must recognize that the federal government forms an essential part of America's money media. You must pay attention to it for your own financial well-being.

If you prefer fixed returns on your investments, you likely already deal, directly or indirectly, with the federal government. Even if you don't, Washington determines the stability of your bank, the rate you pay on a home mortgage, the state of the stock market, the taxes you pay and many other things of import to you and your family.

WORLD BIGGEST SECURITIES FIRM

Uncle Sam operates a giant financial business which dwarfs brokerage giants like Merrill Lynch. Its Treasury Department finances the federal government, dealing in treasury bills, notes and bonds at wholesale and at retail, working through the nation's banks.

If you invest, you are likely to eventually hold some of these securities in your portfolio. You also may draw interest from such government guaranteed mortgage lending securities as the Government Home Loan Mortgage Association (Ginnie Mae) and the Federal Home Loan Mortgage Corporation (Freddie Mac). You may save some of your money in an IRA or other retirement programs certified by the Internal Revenue Service.

That agency and other commissions, departments, bureaus and offices of the U.S. Government publish tons of informational material. Learning how to use federal data could benefit your portfolio.

HOW GOVERNMENT AFFECTS INVESTING

Tax changes, whether up or down, affect investment profits. Pollution control laws generate an industry for cleaning the environment, and that offers profit opportunities for smart investors. The rebuilding of America's creaking infrastructure with federal money presents other opportunities. So it goes. Market-affecting news emerges steadily from government offices.

Fortunately, you need not hunt hard for any of this information. General publications summarize the facts and figures. Business and financial publications interpret them.

Constant Flow Of Headlines

"INSIDER-TRADING RULES MAY BE STIFFENED," says one headline on a Washington-generated story. "U.S. ECONOMY

GREW 2.6% IN QUARTER," says another. "THRIFT INDUSTRY'S LOSSES FALL SHARPLY," says a third. This all on one day of such headlines!

The Information Volume Grows

The need for speedy information about legislative and bureaucratic moves accelerates as governments expand. The Organization for Economic Cooperation and Development estimates that government spending in member countries increased from 29 percent of Gross Domestic Product in 1960 to 41 percent in 1988. That trend, true in America too, means that government influence on business keeps growing.

ANALYZING THE EFFECTS

The economy sneezes every time the Federal Government coughs. It also gallops ahead when the government loosens the credit flow to the economy.

Negative influences may range from taxes on capital gains to reductions in infrastructure spending. Congress and the Federal Reserve Board can create economic panics, too. Both cooperated (though not intentionally) to cause that October 19, 1987, stock market collapse. Earlier, the Board squeezed money growth for months, setting the charge for the market fall. Congressman Dan Rostenkowski lit the fuse by suggesting a need for legislation to control corporate takeovers. Such buy-outs supported that booming stock market. The threat to them destroyed investors' confidence, and the market collapsed in a heap.

Investors have long recognized that actions by the Federal Reserve, by Congressmen or by any other part of the government can indeed strongly affect markets. Thus, they watch Washington with all the vigilance displayed by a sentinel on the outer edges of a defense redoubt under constant attack.

Positive influences might include tax reductions, an easier credit policy or a wave of contracts to federal suppliers. Elimination of the capital gains tax means a big plus for the economy and for the stock market. Reductions in both the federal budget and the trade deficit also rank high among favorable factors.

THE BUSINESS OF GOVERNMENT

Bureaucrats and legislators spout an endless volume of orders, new interpretations, reports, statistics and press statements. One day, the Securities and Exchange Commission interprets the meaning of insider trading for investors. The same day, the IRS may explain application of a tax measure, and a foreign trade report from the Department of Commerce may emerge alongside a study analyzing projected Defense Department spending cuts.

THE COMMERCE DEPARTMENT

The Commerce Department plays a major role in the barrage of information. Officials fight unfair foreign trade competition. Statisticians provide social and economic data and analyses for business and government planners. Specialists grant patents and register trademarks.

Maritime experts in the department foster development of the U.S. Merchant Marine. Tourism authorities promote travel to the United States. Various offices support the increased use of scientific, engineering and technological developments.

A Newsmaker

With such a charter, the department regularly makes news. It issues dozens of statistical tabulations on a monthly, quarterly and annual basis. Wall Streeters watch for them, analyze the data and draw interpretations for managing investments.

The quarterly Gross National Product reports, for instance, measure this country's economic health. Declines forecast industrial and marketing troubles, with repercussions for shareholders. A gain in the GNP index heralds an economic upturn. However, if the gain occurs with full employment and humming factories, it telegraphs an overheating of the economy. That could mean inflation. The stock market will react accordingly.

The Index of Leading Economic Indicators

The Index of Economic Indicators ranks high as a market tool among investment professionals. The Commerce Department constructs it monthly by combining twelve different categories of statistics for one overall figure. Included are: the Federal Reserve's money supply data; an index of raw materials prices; new claims for unemployment insurance; the volume of new consumer goods orders; the dollar level of capital goods orders; the level of business inventories; loans outstanding to business and consumers; the number of building permits for new housing; a tabulation of new business starts; the average length of the work week in industry; the level of the Standard & Poor's 500 stock index; and the amount of supplier order delays reported by manufacturers.

Investors draw little value from minor changes up or down in that index when the various elements show conflicting trends. However, if a majority of those components trend in one direction, this may forecast the future pace of the economy. Moreover, popular wisdom says that should that index decline for three successive months, then we face recession.

Commerce's Publications

The Commerce Department's Bureau of Economic Analysis makes available on a subscription basis a monthly publication that provides statistical pictures of the U.S. economy: *The Survey of Current Business*. It looks beyond the spot news stories, providing data for much deeper analysis.

Statistics and articles in the publication concern capacity utilization, industrial production, money data and much more. For subscription, contact The Public Information Office, Bureau of Economic Analysis, Department of Commerce, Washington, DC, 20230. Many libraries also subscribe to this publication.

THE FEDERAL TRADE COMMISSION (FTC)

You can benefit also from the consumer protection activities of the FTC. It combats credit abuses and unfair trade practices and warns investors of frauds. A copy of the Commission's list of publications is available free—write to The Division of Legal and Public Records, Federal Trade Commission, Washington, DC, 20580.

Coin collectors may already have the Commission's "consumer alert" on investing in rare coins. The Commission published this jointly with the American Numismatic Association. The brochure discusses grading abuses and some of the misrepresentations found in the coin field. If interested in a free copy, write directly to ANA at 818 N. Cascade Ave., Colorado Springs, CO, 80903. If you suspect you have been bilked in coins, contact the FTC in Washington.

THE FEDERAL RESERVE

Interest rate movement and credit action emanate from the Federal Reserve Board. Anytime rates rise, assume that the stock market will falter. Should rates ease, Wall Street regards this as bullish for shares. The market does not *always* surge in tandem with those interest changes, but it pays to understand the usual cause-effect relationship. (Refer to the Three Step And Stumble rule described in Chapter 9.) Fed action seldom comes without warnings from financial publications. Even your daily newspaper likely will inform you when the Fed acts. If you happen to be buying a house, your banker probably will closely monitor Fed activity which could affect your mortgage rate—something which you, too, should consider.

The Federal Reserve Bank of New York publishes an excellent, free, thirty-two-page primer for fixed-income investors, *The Arithmetic of Interest Rates*. Obtain information about federal securities from the free booklet, *Buying Treasury Securities at Federal Reserve Banks*. Write the Federal Reserve Bank of Richmond, Public Service Department, Box 27622, Richmond, VA 23261.

To obtain application blanks for purchase of Treasury securities by mail, write to the Bureau of Public Debt, Division of Customer

Services, Washington, DC, 20239. Obtain Information about all Fed publications from Publications Office, Room MP-510, Martin Building, Federal Reserve System, Washington, DC, 20551 or call (202) 452 3244.

THE DEPARTMENT OF ENERGY

Government data flows steadily from the Energy Information Administration of the Department of Energy on coal, oil, gas and other energy sources. The Bureau of Mines collects, compiles, analyzes and publishes information on all phases of mineral resources development.

THE INTERNAL REVENUE SERVICE

Don't overlook the Internal Revenue Service (IRS), either. Its free brochures help you manage your IRAs. One provides guidance in handling a lump sum from your employer, either at retirement or when changing jobs. Obtain a list of free IRS publications from your local office or that to which you file returns.

THE BUREAU OF THE CENSUS

The Bureau of the Census issues much material of worth to investors who understand the importance of demographic trends to the economy. (According to Artemus Ward, a 19th century humorist, all the Bureau does is ask questions like: "Did you ever have the measles, and if so how many?") Not true, of course. Who hasn't heard about the Baby Boom of the late 1940s and the resulting population bulge, which still appears throughout America's population? With Census figures, economists followed this group from the cradle to midlife as Baby Boomers became Yuppies. Investors who recognized early the economic effects of the bulge profited greatly.

The Graying Of America

Every population count produces data with ideas for investors. The graying of America is one example. Since 1970, the share of Americans over age 64 increased by nearly 45 percent. The proportion will grow another 20 percent by the end of this century. Thus, senior citizens create business for travel and financial companies. Nursing home chains expand. Advertisements for false teeth cleaners, self-analyzing health devices, arthritis remedies and similar products appear on television.

Stocks of drug companies like Bristol-Myers, Forest Laboratories, Marion Laboratories, Abbott Laboratories and scores of others zoomed upward along with the senior population growth. In 1980, Marion Labs stock sold for 70 cents a share, considering splits. In 1989, Dow Chemical offered $38 a share for it.

Interpreting The Data

Investors, however, must interpret population trends very carefully before reacting to them. Certainly, stocks of hospital and nursing home chains like Beverly Enterprises, Manor Care or National Medical Enterprises did benefit mightily. Then, the Federal Government, through Medicare, tightened controls on rising medical costs. Company earnings dropped and some nursing home chains slashed services so deeply that they ran afoul of state laws. Shares of many medical suppliers plunged. Beverly Enterprise stock fell to a low of $3.75 in 1989, far below its peak of $22.50 reached in 1986. Manor Care stock in the same year hovered around 60 percent of the $25.50 reached in 1985.

Obviously, you not only must move early into shares benefiting from a demographic trend, you also must recognize the time to sell. Good information helps with those decisions.

Today, several population trends are emerging. Enrollments are declining in secondary schools, while four million more kids will enter elementary classes in the next ten years. Sales of high school class rings will drop. Younger kids will need more educational tools.

Everybody knows that more women are taking jobs. That means that women today cook fewer meals at home than did their mothers. Meanwhile, two paychecks in a family encourage dining out. Voila! Restaurant chains thrive. Early in the 1960s, people ate one meal in five in restaurants. Today, the average family eats one meal in three there.

Meanwhile, fewer teenagers enter the labor market. Already McDonald's, Denny's and other fast food chains feel the resulting labor pinch. Temporary-help companies fill part of the gap with senior citizens. So employment firms like Olsten Corp., Kelly Services and Adia Services thrive.

A Helpful Source

Investors, indeed, do profit from census statistics if they interpret trends correctly and quickly. A magazine like *American Demographics* (Box 68, Ithaca, NY, 14851) eases the task. It analyzes raw population data and explains consequences to readers.

Some investors also like the Census Bureau's *City and County Data Book*. The 964-page work contains much information about local government finances, employment, vital statistics, income and such. The volume incorporates data from the Census and from fifteen other public and private organizations. To buy copies, contact the Public Information Office, Bureau of the Census, Department of Commerce, Washington, DC, 20233.

INFORMATION AGENCIES

The government's information center in Colorado compiles quarterly lists of over 200 federal publications of consumer interest. Topics cover a wide range, including money management. Obtain a free catalog and get on their mailing list (write to Consumer Information Center, Consumer Catalog, Pueblo, CO, 81009).

If you experience trouble with any commodity trade, seek help from the Commodity Futures Trading Commission at 2033 K St., N.W., Washington, DC, 20581.

The Government Manual

What with the money media maintaining constant vigils, people need not call government offices for information about financial developments. But suppose you need a federal contact? The latest issue of *The United States Government Manual* tells you where to turn.

This 900-page annual lists and describes all federal agencies. Included are names, titles, addresses and phone numbers of key officials. Organizational charts outline functions. The Office of the Federal Register of the General Services Administration, (Washington, DC, 20408) publishes the volume. Purchase it from the Superintendent of Documents, U.S. Government Printing Office, Washington, DC, 20402.

This office also distributes other publications from departments and bureaus of the Federal Government. This includes the Bureau of the Census' *Statistical Abstract of the U.S.*, its *Pocket Data Book, U.S.A.*, its *Bureau of the Census Catalog* and its *Historical Statistics of the United States, Colonial Times to 1970.*

It also sells Bureau of Economic Analysis publications, including: *The Survey of Current Business, Business Statistics, Business Conditions Digest, Area Economic Projections, The National Income and Product Accounts of the United States, Handbook of Cyclical Indicators* and *Local Area Personal Income.* From the International Trade Administration comes another publication, *Business America.*

Information on publications of the government (plus answers to questions of general interest) may be available at Federal Information Centers around the country. These operate in forty-one major metropolitan areas. Usually the Centers occupy Federal Buildings. Telephone numbers are to be found under United States Federal Government listings in phone books.

EVALUATING DATA

Government information seldom points in one direction. You must constantly evaluate what you receive, noting all angles.

"FARM PRICES DECLINE," claims an Agricultural Department study. So farmer spending will drop, too. Retailers could suffer, but consumers may benefit through lower prices. Food companies' shares should rise while agricultural equipment stocks falter.

"U.S. PERSONAL INCOME POSTS HEALTHY GAIN," claims the Commerce Department. Good news for retailers and the economy! But on the same day, the Federal Reserve Board reports "a slower pace of economic growth," a bearish statement. Actually, financial markets rallied. Wall Street estimated the Fed would not hike interest rates in a growth slowdown, for fear of hurting the stock market. So professionals viewed the news favorably.

The Commerce Department's monthly report of Personal Disposable Income informs retailers about the pocketbook strength of customers. Should PDI decline over a few months, shares of merchandisers likely face weakness, too. As marketers reduce orders, manufacturers join the slump.

Corporate Profits Count

The Commerce Department issues its Corporate Profits report quarterly. Profits fuel share price climbs. Ford Motor reported a profit of $4.54 a share in 1985, one of over $11 in 1988. In that period, its share price tripled. After years of red ink, Bank of America showed a $4 per share profit in 1988. Its share price doubled by 1989 from $9.50 a share in 1985.

So it goes. Corporate profits decisively affect share prices, though stocks of individual companies may lag behind earnings at various times.

The Wall Street Journal publishes its own corporate profits report a month after each quarter ends. That beats the government's statistics by three weeks, so market watchers pay close attention to that, too. So should you as an investor.

TRADE ASSOCIATIONS

Trade associations operate independently of government. However, they add to the data flowing from Washington because many are headquartered there. They too produce studies bearing on the economy, whether or not they originate in the nation's capital.

Each month, the National Machine Tool Builders Association tabulates machine tool orders, statistics worthwhile for estimating capital goods trends. The Insurance Services Office and the National Association of Independent Insurers publish quarterly reports of profits of property and casualty companies. These provide clues to insurance stock movements.

Hundreds of trade associations issue pertinent data. Monthly auto sales statistics help predict profits of car makers. Mortgage banker tabulations indicate the pace of home building. This also affects the lumber, cement, furniture and appliance industries, among others. Reports of the National Association of Purchasing Managers reveal manufacturing price trends.

All that information lies at your fingertips, available to help you make money with your investments. Combine the mass of information from all sources, then postulate the possible effects on investment markets and upon your particular stocks. As writer W. Somerset Maugham rightly remarked: "It is a great nuisance that knowledge can only be acquired by hard work."

The Money Media Helps

The business press and investment letters thrive on your need for information. Many of us are like Dorothy Parker, the writer and wit, who said, when deprecating her memory: "I might repeat to myself, slowly and soothingly, a list of quotations beautiful from minds profound; if I can remember any of the damn things."

If your temperament doesn't blend well with research, let someone else make sense from the often disparate government or trade association information. *Changing Times* Magazine has been a data interpreter for decades. *The Wall Street Journal, Business Week,* and *Forbes* are others.

The *New York Times* showed how well the press may interpret government actions and consequences in one story by Sarah Bartlett in December, 1988. Her story appeared at the culmination of the bitter battle for control of RJR Nabisco Inc. In it, she explained how a company priced by the stock market at $55 a share could sell for $109 per share shortly after.

Public markets misinterpreted the true value of corporate assets, she wrote. Management tried to steal the company from under the noses of its shareholders. Wall Street, steeped in greed and ego, overbid for RJR Nabisco, she added.

She also blamed the Federal Government for allowing the deduction of interest while taxing company dividends. That makes debt more attractive than equity for raising capital to take over a corporation. So America experienced a wave of corporate takeovers which may do more harm than good.

The money media also warns investors of scams which may lighten pocketbooks considerably. How to avoid some of them merits a closer look in the next and final chapter.

Chapter 14

Avoiding Scams And Shaping Profit Strategies

Jerry Brown, California's ex-governor and one-time presidential candidate, looked every inch the politician staging a comeback after being elected chairman of the California State Democratic Party. Stepping to the podium in the Sacramento hall, he greeted enthusiastic well-wishers with the platitudes of thanks which roll so easily from lips of most vote seekers.

But Brown is not your usual politician. He leavens any speech with a scholar's erudition, employing metaphors and figures of speech (which mean something to himself, if not to many others). In this speech, he startled the assembly with his neology as he called for all Democrats to "tangibilitize" their support for the party. Listeners exchanged questioning glances; the pencils of news reporters hung suspended over their notebooks. But nobody ran for a dictionary, because Brown provided an explanation immediately.

"You know what it means? It means you have to send us a check. It means you have to make your commitment tangible," he said. Smiles appeared. Now, the new chairman found himself on the same wavelength as the party members in attendance—everybody knows that a political party always needs money.

EVERYBODY WANTS YOUR MONEY

Politicians aren't alone in this respect. Today, it seems that every-body wants a check, no matter what the cause. That goes double in the investing sphere. As an investor, you must learn early how to say "no" in a loud voice.

Scams Abound

Information helps you profit from your financial commitments, but it can't replace plain common sense. Don't "tangibilitize" opportunities offered by phone calls from strangers selling gold bars, collectible coins, high return second mortgages, a hot stock, real estate or anything else which supposedly pays tremendous returns.

Nelson Algren, the late Chicago writer who covered the seamy side, once said: "Never play cards with a man named Doc." Such characters likely deal from the bottom of the deck, as do numerous "Docs" in the telephone solicitation shops of finance.

Those supposedly rich oil wells sold by phone seldom gush any more than water even if promoters really do drill with your money. Precious gems "guaranteed" to protect you against inflation may be only pretty stones. Coins, gold concentrate, strategic metals, mines, art work, penny stocks—you name it! Shysters ply you with such offers, striving to grab your attention on a phone or, less likely, face-to-face. Each year, Americans lose $10 billion to con artists, gaining only bitter experiences from their "investments."

GETTING EDUCATED

Learn more about this issue from *Investor Alert! How to Protect Your Money from Schemes, Scams and Frauds*. The Council of Better Business Bureaus and the North American Securities Administrators Association published it. Bookstores may carry it; if not, reach the Council at Dept. 023, Washington, DC, 20042-0023.

The Council also sells another worthwhile publication, *Tips on Avoiding Telemarketing Fraud*. The Securities and Exchange Commission offers a free publication for investors: *Beware of Penny Stock*

Fraud. Write for it to Office of Consumer Affairs, SEC, 450 Fifth St., Mail Stop 2-6, NW, Washington, DC, 20549. For checking the trust-worthiness of a company, contact your nearest Better Business Bureau.

Check Your Bank, Too

With banks and savings and loans beset by crisis, you can benefit by being careful about where you open accounts. For example, you can order customized safety reports on three banks or savings and loans of your choice from *The Holt Advisory*, Weiss Research, Inc., Box 2923, West Palm Beach, FL, 33402.

Weiss Research also publishes *Money & Markets*. This monthly contains a "Bank Safety Monitor" section which updates readers concerning safety of area banks.

SUCCESSFUL INVESTORS NEED DISCIPLINE

When it comes to investing, adopt a gambler's technique for your protection. Gambler Nick the Greek (Nicholas Dandalos) once said: "The secret and the difference between winners and losers is in discipline. The winner manages his money. The loser lets the money manage him (or her)." He probably envisioned a poker game or crap tables when he said that. Nevertheless, his philosophy applies to investing, too. Risks exist every time you put money to work. You gamble that profit opportunities outweigh the risks.

Develop the discipline to say "no" to possible scams and to questionable solicitations. Strengthen your resolve for *all* of your financial dealings. Coolly measure the risks connected with any deal, then study the profit potential while suppressing any "get-rich-quick" impulses stimulated by promoters.

Do Financial Planners Help?

With all the risks around, you might welcome the help (at a price) of a financial planner or a money manager. The first studies your goals, income and assets, then tells you how to reshuffle your holdings. The second manages your investments, with the best operating with minimums of $100,000 or more.

A good planner or manager may make money for you. They all multiply your risks, since they bear watching, too. If you gather enough data from the money media to make yourself an insider, you shouldn't need an outsider to handle (or mishandle) your money.

INVESTMENT GOALS

Your investment goals should be:

- to protect your capital;
- to guard against inflation; and
- to earn a fair return.

Protecting Your Capital

You protect your capital by avoiding as much risk as you can. Remember, though, that profits depend upon your taking some risks. Generally, no risk equals no profit. Even a "safe" investment in United States Treasury bonds faces danger from inflation.

In periods of high inflation, you lose money in most fixed rate securities. With stocks, the companies may not meet earnings expectations. With real estate, the market could collapse as it did in Texas in the 1980s when oil prices fell. So ascertain how much risk you can tolerate and still sleep at night. Develop an investment strategy which keeps you within your risk perimeters. Don't risk anything that you cannot afford to lose.

Your risk level decreases with age. At twenty-two, you fear little, including the possibility of being wiped out by a foolhardy investment. You know you can always come back. After thirty or thirty-five, you lose some of that assurance, but still take a few chances. At fifty-five, caution reigns, with only a few exceptions.

Although you always hear of bulls and bears in markets, be a chicken with your own money. Aim to get rich slowly, not to make quick killings. The law of compound return (see Chapter 8) works well for patient investors.

Fighting Inflation

Never overlook the dangers of inflation, either. Wise investors follow the Commodity Research Bureau's spot index of twenty-three commodities to gauge inflation trends. Long-term bond prices usually plummet when inflation receives front-page coverage in the news. Stocks follow, though not in tandem. *The Wall Street Journal* and *Investor's Daily* publish that index in every issue, as does the weekly *Barron's*. So do the business sections of numerous daily newspapers.

In your investment return computations, always add inflation's effects. If you earn 10 percent from a bond, with the government's cost of living at 6 percent, your real rate of return is 4 percent. That true rate puts a different face upon any profit you might be estimating.

Look for a Fair Return

You certainly do want a fair return from your holdings. However, what is considered "fair" varies with different situations, interest rate changes, economic conditions and such. The rate on long-term Treasury bonds provides a good benchmark to determine what is fair, even as it rises and falls. These securities are the safest in the world. If you take risks which exceed those experienced when holding Treasuries, then you should expect a higher return on the investment. In 1989, when long-term Treasuries were around 8 percent, investors could obtain 9 percent from certificates of deposit and 10 percent from commercial paper. Knowledgeable equity investors sought a minimum average of 12 percent or 15 percent from stocks, with estimated appreciation and dividends.

With a little practice and some help from your many information sources, you can measure the risks and possible returns of other investments against Treasuries.

DEVELOP AN INVESTMENT STRATEGY

To increase your chances of earning profits, develop an investment strategy. Knowledge acquired through information helps. Information accumulates all around you; knowledge is acquired after you sift through information to formulate a plan of action.

Setting Targets

Begin by asking yourself a few questions. What are your aims concerning investing, i.e., to send a child to college, to purchase a home, to prepare for retirement? You may aim at several different targets, or concentrate on one. Different goals require different strategies.

If you want to protect your current holdings above everything else, hard assets, such as gold, silver and real estate may appeal more than do equities. If you need housing for your family, you start with real estate. If you save for the education of your children, zero coupon bonds or federal EE bonds might appeal. If you are faced with a high tax bill, your strategy aims at minimizing payments to the IRS.

INVESTMENT METHODS

What investment methods will you use to manage your money? Will you depend on fundamental information, technical analysis or both? Will you focus on fixed return investments, i.e., certificates of deposit, Ginnie Maes and other mortgage paper, direct purchase bonds, commercial paper? Do you prefer investing in equities, in real estate, in limited partnerships?

You can reduce risk through diversification, but do you have a large enough stake to do so? Maybe you should concentrate on one or more mutual funds.

Plan your strategy for a period of years and stick to the program. Certainly strategies may change with time. Value investors who buy extremely cheap stocks when others don't want them may move carefully into money funds as the prices of their stocks creep upward. At the peak of a bull market, such investors may be entirely in money funds.

Generally, though, the average investor does not time markets very well. Even a star performer like Peter Lynch, retired manager of the $9 billion Magellan Fund, admits he can't guess when a market will top or hit bottom. So he doesn't try. He looks for stocks which fit his particular fundamental strategy and he holds them for as long as they meet his criteria.

Learn When To Sell

As part of your strategy, learn when to sell by listening to the experts' advice. Unfortunately, many advisors, especially among brokers, tell you when to buy; scarcely any of them advise you when to sell. If their comments confuse you, use the rate of return on the investment as your sell signal. Without any dividend increase, that return declines if the price soars. With a blue chip stock, your rule of thumb might be to sell when the dividend slumps to a ten-year low as the stock's price outruns dividend increases.

With stocks which pay no dividends, sell when earnings falter, unless you possess inside information which suggests otherwise. Move fast, too, because Wall Street professionals rush for the exits with such stocks.

INVESTING PITFALLS TO AVOID

Traps exist to catch careless investors, and they do not all involve scams. Investment professionals list numerous mistakes often made by investors when in the market. Among them:

- Falling in love with particular stocks.
- Approaching investing as if the market were a casino.
- Acting on the basis of "hot" tips.
- Ignoring the homework necessary for stock evaluation.
- Selling winners too soon, keeping losers too long.

- Following the crowd instead of bucking it.
- Dealing in something you don't know.
- Trading rather than investing.
- Buying low-priced "dogs," believing they lead to riches.
- Being greedy for profit, or overcautious about risk.

If any of these propensities apply to you, correct your mistakes before they cost you money.

If a friend in the computer industry tells you hiring slumps at his place of employment, look into it. This could indicate a business slowdown, with consequences on your investments. Pay attention, also, to the little things of life. Information garnered from some of those situations might bolster your profits or reduce your losses. When shopping, if you encounter shortages in any item, investigate who makes the product and reasons for its popularity. Maybe that company's stock should be in your portfolio. Then, again, if manufacturing problems cause the delays, its stock might better be avoided.

Always Be Open to Information

The information accumulation never ends. You can't learn too much about markets and the shares traded on them. Everywhere you turn, you find talkative individuals, new publications and additional sources of information for investing.

One well regarded letter, *TJFR, Business News Reporter*, looks behind-the-scenes at reporters and editors of financial and business publications. It contains fascinating stories behind some of the major financial developments which shake markets.

Your morning's mail may bring a promotion for a magazine being introduced into the United States. It offers a charter subscription to the new publication, *Billion*, which focuses upon business and financial developments in booming Southeast Asia. Stock markets in Thailand, Singapore, Taiwan, South Korea and elsewhere offer tremendous opportunities for investors who acquire information early enough to act upon it. A little thing like the right magazine subscription could lead you to a profitable new investment.

A FINAL WORD

Alistair Cooke, the erudite, octogenarian journalist and television host, bolstered his brilliant career by offering observations on the little things which occur between people. His acute perceptions add an extra dimension of immediacy to any telecast he moderates.

The *New York Times* caught this facet of Cooke's many talents in a piece published in its "Living Arts" section just after the November, 1988, presidential election. It quoted a remark made by the television personality to indicate how small things sometimes become symbolic. Said Cooke: "On the night of the election, I was in a supermarket. I overheard a large, plump woman with a foreign accent say to a small, wizened woman, 'Why, why, why did you vote for Dukakis?' And the wizened lady said very gravely, 'Because 85 percent of the people in prison in the United States were not breast-fed!'"

People often reach for such meaningless rationalizations when pressed for an answer to a question they might not know themselves, explained Cooke.

As the preceding pages have emphasized, you can acquire enough knowledge from investment information sources to prevent your ever having to rationalize a financial decision. The informed investor has a solid reason for every investment choice made, a reason which can be expressed clearly should anyone enquire about it.

Your portfolio will yield profits in accordance with a systematic, well considered investment strategy predicated upon information available in the money media—not because 85 percent of the people in prison were not breast-fed in their infancies!

Appendix

List Of Helpful Addresses

AAII Journal, see American Association of Individual Investors

Acker Letter (The), 2718 E. 63rd St., Brooklyn, NY 11234

Aden Analysis, PO Box 523, Bethel, CN 06801

Addison Report, PO Box 402, Franklin, MA 02038

Advertising Age, 220 E. 42nd St., New York, NY 10017

Advest Group, Inc., 6 Central Row, Hartford, CT 06103

Adweek, 49 E. 21st St., New York, NY 10010

Agora, Inc., 824 E. Baltimore St., Baltimore, MD 21202

AIC Investment Bulletin, 7 North St., Pittsfield, MA 01201

AIQ Systems Inc., 1-800/332-2999

American Association of Individual Investors, 625 N. Michigan Ave., Chicago, IL 60611-9737

American Banker, One State Street Plaza, New York, NY 10004

American Broadcasting Companies Inc., 77 W. 66th St., New York, NY 10023

Note: Addresses correct at time of printing.

American Demographics, Box 68, Ithaca, NY 14851

American Media Group, Inc., 951 Broken Sound Parkway N.W., PO Box 3007, Boca Raton, FL 33431-0907

American Numismatic Association, 818 N. Cascade Ave., Colorado Springs, CO 80903

American Stock Exchange, 86 Trinity Place, New York, NY 10006-1881

American Stock Exchange Weekly, see above address

Amex Handbook, see Standard & Poor's

Analysis & Outlook, PO Box 1167, Port Townsend, WA 98368

Analyst's Handbook, see Standard & Poor's

Argus Research, 17 Battery Place, New York, NY 10004

Asset International Inc., 18 Desbrosses St., New York, NY 10013

Aviation Week & Space Technology, McGraw Hill, Inc., 1120 Vermont Ave., Suite 1200, Washington, DC 20005-3533

Babson-United Investment Advisors, Inc., 101 Prescott St., Wellesley Hills, MA 02181-3319

Bank & Finance Manual, see Moody's

Bank Credit Analyst, BCA Publications Ltd., Box 238, Chazy, NY 12921

Bank Safety Monitor, Weiss Research, Inc., P.O. Box 2923, West Palm Beach, FL 33402

Bankers Monthly, 200 W. 57th St., 15th Fl., New York, NY 10019

Barron's, Dow Jones & Co., 200 Liberty St., New York, NY 10281

Barron's Finance & Investment Handbook, Barron's Educational Series, Inc., 250 Wireless Blvd., Hauppauge, NY 11788

Bear, Stearns & Co., 245 Park Ave., New York, NY 10167

Beef, The Webb Co., 1999 Shepard Rd., St. Paul, MN 55116

Better Business Bureaus (Council of), 1515 Wilson Blvd., Arlington, VA 22209 (For publications, write Council at Dept. 023, Washington, DC 20042-0023)

Better Investing, Box 220, Royal Oak, MI 48068

Billion, Sing Tao Ltd., Hong Kong, American contact: David Tinnin, 301 Henry St., Lindenhurst, NY 11757-9864

BI Research, PO Box 133, Redding, CT 06875

Blanchard (James U.) & Co., 2400 Jefferson Hwy., Jefferson, LA 70121

Blue Chip Economic Indicators, Capital Publications, 1300 N. 17th St., Arlington, VA 22209

Blue Chip Financial Forecasts, PO Box 1454, Alexandria, VA 22313

Blue List, see Standard & Poor's

Bob Nurock's Advisory, PO Box 988, Paoli, PA 19301

Bond Buyer, One State Street Plaza, New York, NY 10004

Bond Fund Survey, Survey Publications Co., Grand Central Station, Box 4180, New York, NY 10163

Bond Fund Timer, PO Box 360, Bellmore, NY 11710

Bond Guide, see Standard & Poor's

Bond Holders News Letter, Financial Government, 6011 Blaine Rd., NW, Washington, DC 20011

Bond Investors Association, 5979 N.W. 151st St., #240, Miami Lakes, FL 33014, tele. 1-305/557-1832

Bond Market Report, Gabriele Hueglin & Cashman, 44 Wall Street, New York, NY 10005

Bond Record and *Survey*, see Moody's

Bond Traders Guide, see Vickers Stock Research Corp.

Bondweek, Institutional Investor, Inc., 488 Madison Ave., New York, NY 10022

Boston Business Journal, MCP Publishers, 451 D. St., Boston, MA 02210-1907

Boston Globe, Globe Newspaper Co., 135 Morrissey Blvd., Boston, MA 02107

Bowser Report, PO Box 6278, Newport News, VA 83606

Breakthrough Publishing, PO Box 5600, San Ramon, CA 94583-5600

Brown (Kenneth) Market Letter, 980 N. Federal Hwy, Suite 101, Boca Raton, FL 33432

Browne's (Harry) Special Reports, PO Box 5586, Austin, TX 78763

Browning Newsletter, Fraser Management Assoc. Inc., PO Box 494, Burlington, VT 05402

Bullish Consensus (The), Hadady Corporation, 1111 S. Arroyo Pkwy., Pasadena, CA 91109-0490

Bureau of the Census, Information Office, Department of Commerce, Washington, DC 20333

Bureau of Economic Analysis (U.S.), Public Information Office, BEA, Department of Commerce, Washington, DC 20230

Bureau of Mines (U.S.), Office of Technical Information, BM, Department of the Interior, 2401 E St., NW, Washington, DC 20241

Business America, U.S. Department of Commerce, 14th St., & Constitution Ave. NW, Rm. 3414, Washington, DC 20230

Business and Investment Almanac (Dow Jones-Irwin), see Dow Jones-Irwin

Business Atlanta, Communication Channels Inc., 6255 Barfield Rd., Atlanta, GA 30328

"Business Day," see Cable News Network

Business Forecasts, Weiss Research, 2206 Florida Margold, West Palm Beach, FL 33409

Business Month, Goldhirsh Publishing, 488 Madison Ave., New York, NY 10022

"Business Morning," see Cable News Network

Business View, Florida Business Publications Inc., Box 9859, Naples, FL 33941

Business Week, McGraw-Hill, Inc., 1221 Avenue of the Americas, New York, NY 10020

"Business World," see American Broadcasting Co.

Buying Treasury Securities at Federal Reserve Banks, Federal Reserve Bank of Richmond, Public Service Dept., Box 27622, Richmond, VA 23261

Cable News Network, One CNN Center, Box 105366, Atlanta, GA 30348-5366

Cable TV Investors' Charts, Paul Kagan Associates, 126 Clock Tower Pl., Carmel, CA 93923

Cabot Market Letter and *Cabot Mutual Fund Navigator,* PO Box 3044, Salem, MA 01970

California Business, 4221 Wilshire Blvd., Suite 400, Los Angeles, CA 90010

California Technology Stock Letter, Suite 1401, 155 Montgomery St., San Francisco, CA 94111

Callard Report On Warranted Values, PO Box 11324, Chicago, IL 60611

Called Bond Record, see Standard & Poor's

Cattleman Magazine, Texas & Southwestern Cattle Raisers Assn., 1301 W. Seventh St., Fort Worth, TX 76102

CBS Inc., 51 W. 52nd St., New York, NY 10019

Changing Times, 1729 H St. NW, Washington, DC 20006

Chartcraft, Inc., 30 Church St., New Rochelle, NY 10801

Chartist (The), PO Box 758, Seal Beach, CA 90740

Chartwatch, 345 N. Canal, Chicago, IL 60606

Chemical Business, Schnell Publishing Co., 80 Broad St., New York, NY 10004

Chemical Week, McGraw Hill, Inc., 1221 Avenue of the Americas, New York, NY 10020

Chicago Board of Trade, 141 W. Jackson Blvd., Chicago, IL 60604

Chicago Mercantile Exchange, 30 S. Wacker Dr., Chicago, IL 60606

Chicago Tribune, 435 N. Michigan Ave., Chicago, IL 60611

Cisco, Commodities Information Services Co., 327 S. LaSalle St., Suite 800, Chicago, IL 60604

Citicorp, 399 Park Ave., New York, NY 10043

Cleveland Plain Dealer, 1801 Superior Ave., N.E., OH 44114

Closed-End Fund Digest, 1280 Coast Village, Circle C, Santa Barbara, CA 93108, tele. 1-800/282-2335

Closed-End Fund Report, Cole Publications, Inc., PO Box 17800, Richmond, VA 23226, tele. 1-800/356-3508

CNBC, 2200 Fletcher Ave., Fort Lee, NJ 07024

CNN, see Cable News Network

Coin and Bullion Dealer Accreditation Program, 25 E St. NW, Eighth Floor, Washington, DC 20001

Coin Enthusiast's Journal, Masongate Publishing, Box 1383, Torrance, CA 90505

Coins, Krause Publications, 700 E. State St., Iola, WI 54990

Coin World, Box 150, Sidney, OH 45365

Collector-Investor, 740 N. Rush St., Chicago, IL 60611

COMEX Reports, see Commodity Exchange

Commerce Clearing House, Inc., 2700 Lake Cook Rd., Riverwoods, IL 60015

Commercial and Financial Chronicle, National News Service, Inc., 5 Beekman St., #728, New York, NY 10038

Commercial Paper Ratings Guide, see Standard & Poor's

Commodities Magazine, 219 Parkade, Cedar Falls, IA 50613

Commodity Chart Service, 75 Montgomery St., Jersey City, NJ 07302

Commodity Exchange, Inc. (COMEX), 4 World Trade Center, New York, NY 10048

Commodity Futures Trading Commission, 2033 K St., N.W., Washington, DC 20581 (handles investor complaints)

Commodity Information Systems, PO Box 690652, Houston, TX 72269

Commodity International Advisor, 141 W. Jackson, Ste. 1765, Chicago, IL 60604

Commodity Journal, American Association of Commodity Traders, 10 Park St., Concord, NH 03301

Commodity Perspective, 30 S. Wacker Dr., Chicago, IL 60606

Commodity Research Bureau, 75 Wall St., New York, NY 10005

Commodity Trader's Almanac, Market Movements Inc., 8236 E. 71st St., Suite 190, Tulsa, OK 74133

Commodity Traders Consumer Reports, 1731 Howe Ave., Suite 149, Sacramento, CA 95825

Commodity Trend Service, 1201 U.S. Hwy. 1, Suite 350, Crystal Tree Plaza, North Palm Beach, FL 33408

Commodity Year Book, see Commodity Research Bureau

Complete Guide To Closed-End Funds, see *Closed-End Fund Digest*

CompuServe, Inc., 5000 Arlington Centre Blvd., Columbus, OH 43220

Compustock, A.S. Gibson & Sons, Inc., 1412 Vineyard Drive, Bountiful, UT 84010

Computer Investor, Man Computer Systems Inc., 84-13 168th St., Jamaica, NY 11432

Computerized Investing, see American Association of Individual Investors

CompuTrac, 1017 Pleasant, New Orleans, LA 70115

ComStock, 670 White Plains Rd., Scarsdale, NY 10583

Comstock Group, 38 Old Ridgebury Rd., Danbury, CO 06810

Confidential Report from Zurich, Export Newsletter Assn., 10076 Boca Entrada Blvd., Box 3007, Boca Raton, FL 33431-0907, tele. 1-305/241-1800

Consensus of Insiders, Box 24349, Fort Lauderdale, FL 33307

Consultant's Certified Coin Report, PO Box 8277, Fountain Valley, CA 92728

Consumer Guide to Financial Independence, see International Association for Financial Planning

Consumer Information Center (U.S.), Dept. RW, Pueblo, CO 81009

Contrarian View (The), 910 Main St., Worcester, MA 01610

Contrary Investor (The), PO Box 494, Burlington, VT 05402

Corporate Registered Bond Interest Record, see Standard & Poor's

Corporation Records, see Standard & Poor's

Council of Better Business Bureaus, 1515 Wilson Blvd., Arlington, VA 22209

Crain's Chicago Business, 740 N. Rush St., Chicago, IL 60611

Crain's Cleveland Business, 700 W. St. Clair Ave., #310, Cleveland, OH 44113

Crain's Detroit Business, Crain Communications, Inc., 1400 Woodbridge, Detroit, MI 48207

CRB Futures Chart Service, Commodity Research Bureau, 75 Wall St., New York, NY 10005

CreditWeek, see Standard & Poor's

Currency Dealer Newsletter, PO Box 11099, Torrance, CA 90510

CUSIP Directories, see Standard & Poor's

Dag (Peter) Investment Letter, 65 Lakefront Dr., Akron, OH 44139

Daily Graphs, PO Box 24933, Los Angeles, CA 90024-0933

Daily Market Comment, PO Box 1234, Pacifica, CA 94044

Daily Stock Price Record, see Standard & Poor's

Daily Trader (The), 110 Boggs Lane, Cincinnati, OH 45246

Davis (Dick) Digest, PO Box 9547, Ft. Lauderdale, FL 33310-9547

Davis (Ned) Research's Stock Market Strategy, 5600 Glenridge Dr., Suite 210, Atlanta, GA 30342

Day's (Adrian) Investment Analyst, PO Box 3217, Silver Spring, MD 20901

Dean Witter Reynolds, PO Box 286, Bowling Green Station, New York, NY 10274-0286

Defaulted Bonds Newsletter, Bond Investors Assn., PO Box 4427, 15327 N.W. 60th Ave., Miami Lakes, FL 33014

Deliberations, PO Box 182, Adelaide St. Sta., Toronto, Ont., Canada M5C2J1

Department of Commerce (U.S.), 14th St., Washington, DC 20230

Department of Energy (U.S.), 1000 Independence Ave., SW. Washington, DC 20585

Department of the Treasury (U.S.), Office of Public Affairs, Washington, DC 20220

Dessauer's Journal, PO Box 1718, Orleans, MA 02653

Dines Letter (The), PO Box 22, Belvedere, CA 94920

Directory of Bond Agents, see Standard & Poor's

Directory of Business and Financial Services, Special Libraries Association, 1700 18th St. N.W., Washington, DC 20402

Directory of Companies Offering Dividend Reinvestment Plans, Evergreen Enterprises, PO Box 763, Laurel, MD 20707 (see also *Moneypaper* for similar directory)

Directory of Companies Required to File Annual Reports (with SEC), U.S. Government Printing Office, Washington, DC 20402

Dividend Record, see Moody's (also see Standard & Poor's)

DJH Analysis, PO Box 977, Crystal Lake, IL 60014

Donoghue Organization (The), 360 Woodland St., Holliston, MA 01746

Donoghue's Money Fund Report, Moneyletter and *Mutual Fund Almanac,* see above listing and address

Dow Jones & Co., 200 Liberty St., New York, NY 10281

Dow Jones Investor's Handbook, Dow Jones-Irwin, 1818 Ridge Rd., Homewood, IL 60430

Dow Jones-Irwin, 1818 Ridge Rd., Homewood, IL 60430 (no connection with Dow Jones & Co.)

Dow Jones News/Retrieval, see Dow Jones & Co.

Dow Theory Forecasts, 7412 Calumet Ave., Hammond, IN 46324-2692

Dow Theory Letters, PO Box 1759, La Jolla, CA 92038

DRI, Commodities Data Bank, Data Resources, 1750 K St., N.W., Suite 1060, Washington, DC 20006

Dun and Bradstreet's Guide to Your Investments, Harper & Row Publishers Inc., 10 E. 53rd St., New York, NY 10022

Earnings Forecaster, see Standard & Poor's

Economist (The), 25 St. James Street, London, England SW1A 1HG

Edwards (A.G.), 1 North Jefferson Ave., St. Louis, MO 63103

Ehrenkrantz Report, 50 Broadway, New York, NY 10004

Eliades' (Peter), Stockmarket Cycles, 2260 Cahuenga Blvd., Suite 205, Los Angeles, CA 90068

Elliott Wave Commodity Forecast (The), Principle Forecast and *Wave Theorist,* New Classics Library, PO Box 1618-B, Gainsville, GA 30503

Emerging & Special Situations, see Standard & Poor's

Emerging Growth Stocks, 7412 Calumet Ave., Hammond, IN 46324

Encyclopedia of Business Information Sources, Gale Research Inc., Book Tower, Detroit, MI 48226

Energy Information Administration (U.S.), Department of Energy, 1000 Independence Ave., SW, Washington, DC 20585

Epstein & Co., 1-800/284-6000

Equity Fund Outlook, PO Box 1040, Boston, MA 02217

Ernest & Whinney Financial Planner Report, PO Box 33337, Washington, DC 20033

ESPN, Entertainment and Sports Program Network, ESPN Plaza, Bristol, CT 06010

Executive Wealth Advisory, National Institute of Business Management, 1328 Broadway, New York, NY 10001

Farm Futures, Agri Data Resources, Inc., 330 E. Kilbourn Ave., Milwaukee, WI 53202

Federal Reserve Bank of New York, 33 Liberty St., New York, N.Y. 10045

Federal Reserve Board, see next item

Federal Reserve System, Office of Public Affairs, Washington, DC 20551 (for brochures contact the Fed's Publications Office, Martin Bldg., Washington, DC 20551)

Federal Trade Commission, Sixth St., and Pennsylvania Ave., NW., Washington, DC 20580

Fidelity Brokerage Services, Inc., 161 Devonshire St., Boston, MA 02110, tele. 1-800/544-6666

Fidelity Insight, see Mutual Fund Investors Association

Fidelity Monitor, PO Box 1294, Rocklin, CA 95677-7294

Finance, 410, rue St. Nichols, #505, Montreal, Quebec H2Y 2P5 Canada

Financial Analysts Journal, 1633 Broadway, New York, NY 10019

Financial Digest, 350 Park Ave., New York, NY 10022

Financial News Network, 6701 Center Drive West, Los Angeles, CA 90045

Financial Strategies, Financial Service Corp., 250 Piedmont Ave. N.E., Suite 1900, Atlanta, GA 30365

Financial Strategist, Blanchard Strategic Growth Fund, 41 Madison Ave., 24th Floor, New York, NY 10010

Financial Times, 14 E. 60th St., New York, NY 10022

Financial World, Financial World Partners, 1450 Broadway, New York, NY 10018

Financier, 420 Lexington Ave., Suite 1739, New York, NY 10170

First American, 1-800/621-4415

First Boston Corp., 20 Exchange Place, New York, NY 10055

Florida Trend, Box 611, St. Petersburg, FL 33731

"FNN Business News," see Financial News Network

Forbes, Forbes, Inc., 60 Fifth Ave., New York, NY 10011

Forbes Special Situation Survey, Forbes Investors Advisory Institute, 60 Fifth Ave., New York, NY 10011

Forecasts & Strategies, see Phillips Publishing

Fortune magazine, Time, Inc., 1271 Ave. of the Americas, New York, NY 10020

Free Market Perspectives, PO Box 471, Barrington Hills, IL 60010

Fuller Money, Chart Analysis Ltd., 7 Swallow St., London W1R 7HD, United Kingdom

Fund Exchange, 1200 Westlake Ave. North, Suite 507, Seattle, WA 98109-3530

Future Economic Trends, 951 Broken Sound Pkwy. N.W., PO Box 3060, Boca Raton, FL 33431-0960

Futures and Options Trader (The), DeLong—Western Publishing Co., 13618 Scenic Crest Drive, Yucaipa, CA 92399

Futures Charts, see Commodity Trend Service

Futures Discount Group

Futures Hotline, PO Box 360, Bellmore, NY 11710, tele. 1-800/633-2252, ext. 9200

Futures magazine, 250 S. Wacker Drive, #1150, Chicago, IL 60606

Futures Market Service, see Commodity Research Bureau

Gabelli Asset, tele. 1-800/422-3554

Generic Stock News, Generic Stock Investment Service, Norstar Bank Bldg., 6th floor, Ithaca, NY 14850

Gerbino (Kenneth) Investment Letter, 9016 Wilshire Blvd., Beverly Hills, CA 90211

Global Investment Outlook Reports, International Executive Reports, 717 D St., N.W., Washington, DC 20004

Goldman Sachs & Co., 85 Broad St., New York, 10004

Gold Mining Stock Report, see *Penny Stock News*

Gold Newsletter, see Blanchard (James)

Gold Show (The), 9100 S. Dadeland Blvd., Suite 702, Miami, FL 33156

Gold Standard News, 1805 Grand Ave., Kansas City, MO 64108

Gordon Market Timer (The), 169 Charlotte Place, Englewood Cliffs, NJ 07632

Grant's Interest Rate Observer, 233 Broadway, Suite 4008, New York, NY 10279-0158

Granville Market Letter (The), PO Drawer 413006, Kansas City, MO 64141

Growth Fund Guide, Box 6600, Rapid City, SD 57709

Growth Stock Advisory, 1101 King St., Suite 400, Alexandria, VA 22314

Growth Stock Outlook, P.O. Box 15381, Chevy Chase, MD 20825

Growth Stock Report, 82 Wall St., Suite 1105, New York, NY 10005

Growth Stocks Handbook, see Standard & Poor's

Guide to Mutual Funds, see American Association of Individual Investors, Donoghue's, Handbook for, Investment Company Institute, Mutual Fund Education Alliance, *Closed-End Fund Digest* and Standard & Poor's

Guinness Book of Records, most bookstores

Handbook Common Stocks and *Handbook OTC Stocks*, see Moody's

Handbook for No-Load Fund Investors (The), Box 283, Hastings-on-Hudson, NY 10706

Hard Money Digest, 3608 Grand Ave., Oakland, CA 94610

Harmonic Research, 650 Fifth Ave., New York, NY 10019

Harvard Business Review, Soldiers Field, Cambridge, MA 02163

Hayes (Tim) Investigative Report, Newsletter Management Corp., 10076 Boca Entrada Blvd., PO Box 3007, Boca Raton, FL 33431-0907

High Tech Stock Handbook, see Standard & Poor's

Holt Advisory (The), Weiss Research, Inc., P.O. Box 2923, West Palm Beach, FL 33402

Horsey (M.C.) & Co., Inc., PO Box H, 120 South Boulevard, Salisbury, Md., 21801, tele. 1-800/633-2252

How to Read a Financial Report, see Merrill Lynch

Hulbert Financial Digest, 316 Commerce St., Alexandria, VA 22314

IDS, Investors Diversified Services, IDS Tower 10, Minneapolis, MN 55440

Income & Safety, see Institute for Econometric Research

Income Stocks Handbook, see Standard & Poor's

Independent Investor (The), Dept. T9A, 161 Devonshire St., Boston, MA 02110

Index Option Advisor, PO Box 46709, Cincinnati, OH 45246, tele. 1-800/228-2028

Indiana Business, 1000 Waterway Blvd., Indianapolis, IN 46202

Indicator Digest, 451 Grand Ave., Palisades Park, NJ 07650

Individual Investor's Guide to Investment Publications, see American Association of Individual Investors

Individual Investor's Guide to No-Load Mutual Funds and *Individual Investor's Microcomputer Resource Guide,* see American Association of Individual Investors

Industrial Manual & News Reports, see Moody's

Industry Review, see Moody's

Industry Surveys, see Standard & Poor's

Innovest Recommendations Service, PO Box 1467, Alexandria, VA 22313

"Inside Business," see Cable News Network

Inside View, N.I.G., Inc., 125 E. Baker, Suite 150, Dept. 20, Costa Mesa, CA 92626

Insider Indicator, 2230 N.E. Brazee St., Portland, OR 97212

Insider Weekly Summary, Invest/Net Group, Inc., 99 N.W. 183 St., North Miami, FL 33169

Insiders (The), see Institute for Econometric Research

Insiders' Chronicle, Financial Information Inc., 398 Camino Garden Blvd., Suite 206, Boca Raton, FL 33432

Insiders' Transactions Report, PO Box 1145, Costa Mesa, CA 92628

Insightful Investor, PO Box 292, Old Westbury, NY 11568

Institute for Econometric Research, 3471 N. Federal Highway, Fort Lauderdale, FL 33306

Institute of Certified Financial Planners, Two Denver Highlands, 10065 E. Harvard Ave., Suite 320, Denver, CO 80231, tele. 1-800/282-7526

Institutional Investor, 488 Madison Ave., New York, NY 10022

Insurance Information Institute, 110 William St., New York, NY 10038

Insurance Investing, PO Box 2090, Huntington Beach, CA 92647

Intelligence Report, see Young's

Interest Rate Forecast, BCA Publications Ltd., Box 238, Chazy, NY 12921

Interest Rate Review, International Institute for Economic Research, PO Box 329, Blackville Rd., Washington Depot, CT 06794

International Advisor (The), WMP Publishing Co., 2211 Lee Rd., Suite 103, Winter Park, FL 32790

International Asset Advisor, Interinvest Corp., Investment Review, Box 1585, Boston, MA 02104

International Assets Advisory Corp., 422 W. Fairbanks, Winter Park, FL 32789

International Association for Financial Planning, Two Concourse Parkway, Suite 800, Atlanta, GA 30328

International Gold Digest, Indicator Research Group, 451 Grand Ave., Palisades Park, NJ 07650

International Gold Report (Young's), Phillips Publishing, 7811 Montrose Rd., Potomac, MD 20854

International Harry Schultz Letter (The), PO Box 622, CH-1001, Lausanne, Switzerland

International Institute for Technical Research, PO Box 338, Blackville Rd., Washington Depot, CT 06794

International Investment Seminars, 10076 Boca Entrade Blvd., PO Box 3007, Boca Raton, FL 33431-0907

International Investor Guide, Asset International, Inc., 18 Desbrosses St., New York, NY 10013

International Manual & News Reports, see Moody's

International Moneyline, 25 Broad St., New York, NY 10004 250 Fifth Ave., Suite 403, New York, NY 10001 also PO Box 58 - 7500 St. Moritz, Switzerland

International Trade Administration, U.S. Department of Commerce, Washington, DC 20230

InvesTech Market Analyst, 2472 Birch Glen, Whitefish, MT 59937

InvesTech Mutual Fund Advisor, 2472 Birch Glen, Whitefish, Mont., 59937, tele. 1-800/955-8500

Investext, 11 Farnsworth St., Boston MA 02210, 1-800/662-7878

Investing in Crisis, 824 E. Baltimore St., Baltimore, MD 21202

Investment Analyst, 824 E. Baltimore St., Baltimore, MD 21202

Investment Clubs of America, see National Association of Investors

Investment Company Institute, 1600 M St. NW, Washington, DC 20036

Investment Dealers Digest, 150 Broadway, New York, NY 10038

Investment Horizons, Investment Information Services, Inc., 680 N. Lake Shore Drive, Tower Suites 2038, Chicago, IL 60611

Investment Management Weekly, Investment Management Publications, 374 Congress St., #504, Boston, MA 02210

Investment Monthly, see KCI Communications,

Investment NewsLetter Directory, Billboard Publications Inc., Larimi Media Directories, 1695 Oak St., Lakewood, NJ 08701, tele. 1-800/336-3533

Investment Newsletters, Public Relations Publishing Inc., 888 Seventh Ave., New York, NY

Investment Quality Trends, 7440 Girard Ave., La Jolla, CA 92037

Investment Reporter, (for Canadian stocks), see Marpep

Investment Seminars, Inc., The Githler Bldg., Second Floor, 1543 Second St., Sarasota, FL 34236, tele. 1-813/955-0323

Investment Strategist, Money Growth Institute Inc., 37 Van Reipen Ave., Jersey City, NJ 07306

Investment Values, Orion Publishing, Inc., PO Box 517, Mt. Kisco, NY 10549

Investment Vision, Fidelity Investments, tele. 1-800/544-6666

Invest/Net Group, 99 N.W. 183 St., North Miami, FL 33169

"Investors Advantage," see Financial News Network

Investor's Daily, circ., Department A, PO Box 25970, Los Angeles, CA 90025-9970

Investor's Guide to Closed End Funds, PO Box 161465, Miami, FL 33116

Investor's Hotline, 10616 Beaver Dam Rd., Suite S-6, Hunt Valley, MD 21030

Investors Intelligence, 30 Church Street, New Rochelle, NY 10801

"Investors News Release Watch," see Financial News Network

Jack Carl/312 Futures, 1-800/621-3424

Janeway Letter (The Eliot Janeway), 15 E. 80th St., New York, NY 10021

Journal of Commerce, 110 Wall Street, New York, NY 10005

Journal of Finance, New York University, 100 Trinity Place, New York, NY 10006

Journal of Portfolio Management, 488 Madison Ave., New York, NY 10022

Journal of Undervalued Stocks (The), Route 706 West, Montrose, PA 18801

Kansas City Board of Trade, 4800 Main St., Suite 303, Kansas City, MO 64112

KCI Communications, Inc., 1101 King St., Suite 400, Alexandria, VA 22314-2980, tele. 1-800/772-9200

Kidder Peabody & Co., 10 Hanover Sq., New York, NY 10005

Klein-Wolman Investment Letter, PO Box 727, Princeton Jct., NJ 08550

Knight-Ridder Trade Center, Department B, One Exchange Plaza, 55 Broadway, New York, NY 10006

Kondratieff Wave Analyst, PO Box 977, Crystal Lake, IL 60014

Laser Focus World, PennWell Publishing Co., Advanced Technology Group, Box 989, Westford, MA 01886

Legg Mason, Inc., 7 E. Redwood St., Baltimore, Md., 21202

Lind-Waldock & Co., 1030 W. Van Buren, Chicago, IL 60607, tele. 1-800/445-2000

Lipper Analytical Services Corp., 74 Trinity Place, New York, NY 10006

Longman, Inc., 95 Church St., White Plains, NY 10601

Los Angeles Times, Times Mirror Square, Los Angeles, CA 90053

Low Price Stock Newsletter, 807 E. South Temple, Salt Lake City, UT 84102

Low Priced Stock Survey (The), Dow Theory Forecasts, Inc., 7412 Calumet Ave., Hammond, ID, 46324-2692

Low-Risk Growth Letter, Kinsman Associates, 255 W. Napa Street, Sonoma, CA 95476, tele. 1-707/935-6504

Lynch International Investment Survey, 301 Main St., Suite 206, Port Washington, NY 11050

Lynch Municipal Bond Advisory, Box 1086, Lenox Hill Station, New York, NY 10021

Managed Account Reports, 5513 Twin Knolls Rd., Suite 213, Columbia, MD 21045

Mansfield Chart Service, 2973 Kennedy Blvd., Jersy City, NJ 07306

Marcum Report, PO Box 606, Geneva, IL 60134

Margo's Market Monitor, PO Box 642, Lexington, MA 02173

Marketarian, 216 N. Cedar, Grand Island, NE 68801

Market Chronicle, 45 John St., New York, NY 10038

Market Express, WMP Enterprises, 3443 Parkway Center Court, Orlando, FL 32808

Market Fax, tele. 415/355-9666

Market Forecaster (The), William Finnegan Associates, Inc., PO Box 1121, Malibu, CA 90265

Market Guide (The), 49 Glen Head Rd., Glen Head, NY 11545

Market Interpreter, Chicago Board of Trade Building, 141 W. Jackson, Chicago, IL 60606

Market Line, 4961 106th St., PO Box 25342, Milwaukee, WI 53225

Market Logic, Institute for Econometric Research, 3471 N. Federal Hwy., Ft. Lauderdale, FL 33306

Market Mania, PO Box 1234, Pacifica, CA 94044

Market Month, see Standard & Poor's

Market Signals, The Northern Trust Company, 150 S. LaSalle St., Chicago, IL 60605

Marketimer, PO Box 7005, Princeton, NJ 08543

Market Vane, 61 S. Lake Ave., Pasadena, CA 91101

Market Vantage, Orion Publishing Co., PO Box.517, Mt. Kisco, NY 10549

"Market Wrapup," see Financial News Network

Marpep Publishing Ltd., 133 Richmond St. W., Toronto, Ontario, Canada M5H 3M8

MBH Letter, MBH Commodity Advisors Inc., PO Box 353, Winnetka, IL 60093

McAlvany Intelligence Advisor, PO Box 84904, Phoenix, AZ 85071

McGraw-Hill, Inc., 1221 Avenue of the Americas, New York, NY 10020

McKeever Strategy Letter, Triversal Marketing, PO Box 4130, Medford, OR 97501, tele. 1-800/237-8400

MECA Ventures, Inc., 355 Riverside Ave., Westport, CT 06880

Media General Inc., 333 E. Grace St., Richmond, VA 23219

Medical Technology Stock Letter, Piedmont Venture Group, PO Box 40460, Berkeley, CA 94704

Memphis Business Journal, 88 Union, Suite 102, Memphis, TN 38103

Merrill Lynch & Co., World Financial Center, North Tower, 250 Vesey Street, New York, NY 10281

MicroAge Quarterly, MicroAge Computer Stores, 2308 S. 55th Street, Tempe, AZ 85282

Mid-America Commodity Exchange, 141 W. Jackson Blvd., Chicago, IL 60604

Midwest Stock Exchange, 440 S. LaSalle St., Chicago, Ill. 60605

MJF Growth Stock Advisory, see KCI Communications

Money & Markets, The Weiss Companies, P.O. Box 2923, West Palm Beach, FL 33402

Money magazine, Money Business Office, Time & Life Bldg., Rockefeller Center, New York, NY 10020-1393

Money's Complete Guide to Personal Finance & Investment Terms, Barron's Educational Series, 250 Wireless Blvd., Hauppauge, NY 11788

Money Digest, Money Digest Press, GPO Box 114, Brooklyn, NY 11202

Money Fund Report, see Donoghue Organization

Money Growth Institute, Inc., 37 Van Reipen Ave., Jersey City, NJ 07306

Money Investors Journal, Institute of Wall Street Studies, Suite 200, 1200 N. Federal Highway, Boca Raton, FL 33432

Moneyletter, see Donoghue Organization

"Moneyline," see Cable News Network

Money Maker Magazine, Consumers Digest Inc., 5705 N. Lincoln Ave., Chicago, IL 60659

Money Manager Review, Smith-Thomas Investment Services, Inc., 770 Tamalpais Drive, Suite 206, Corte Madera, CA 94925

Money Managers Supplement, Vickers Stock Research Corp., Box 59, Brookside, NJ 07926

Moneypaper, 930 Mamaroneck Ave., Mamaroneck, NY 10543

"Moneyweek," see Cable News Network

MoneyWorld, see WMP Enterprises

Moody's Investors Services, 99 Church St., New York, NY 10007

Morgan Stanley Group, Inc., 1251 Avenue of the Americas, New York, NY 10020

MPT Review, PO Box 5695, Incline Village, NV 89450

MultiVest Options Inc., 6151 N.Federal Highway, PO Box 23000, Fort Lauderdale, FL 33307-9983

Muni Bond Fund Report, PO Box 2179, Huntington Beach, CA 92647

Municipal & Govenment Manual, see Moody's

Municipal Registered Bond Interest Record, see Standard & Poor's

Mutual Fund Almanac, see Donoghue Organization

Mutual Fund Advantage, PO Box 4130, Medford, OR 97501

Mutual Fund Education Alliance, 1900 Erie St., Kansas City, MO 64116

Mutual Fund Forecaster, see Institute for Econometric Research

Mutual Fund Investing, see Phillips Publishing

Mutual Fund Investor (The), American River Softwear, 916/483-1600

Mutual Fund Investors Association, PO Box 385, Needham, MA 02192

Mutual Fund Letter (The), Investment Information Services, Inc., Suite 518, 205 W. Wacker Dr., Chicago, IL 60606

Mutual Fund Monitor, 1412 Spruce St., Berkeley, CA 94709

Mutual Fund Profiles see Standard & Poor's

Mutual Fund Specialist, Royal R. Lemier & Co., PO Box 1025, Eau Claire, WI 54702

Mutual Fund Strategist, PO Box 446, Burlington, VT 05402

Mutual Fund Values, 53 W. Jackson Blvd., Chicago, IL 60604

NASDAQ (see National Association of Securities Dealers)

National Association of Independent Insurers, see Insurance Information Institute

National Association of Investors, 1515 E. Eleven Mile Rd., Royal Oak, MI 48067

National Association of Personal Financial Advisors, 1130 Lake Cook Rd., Suite 105, Buffalo Grove, IL 60089, 1-800/366-2732

National Association of Purchasing Managers, 2055 East Centennial Circle, PO Box 22160, Tempe, AZ 85282

National Association of Securities Dealers, 1735 K St., N.W., Washington, DC 20006 (Arbitration Department, 2 World Trade Center, 98th Floor, New York, NY 10048)

National Broadcasting Co., 30 Rockefeller Plaza, New York, NY 10112

National Committee for Monetary Reform, 4425 W. Napoleon Ave., Matairié, LA 70001

National Institute of Business Management, 1328 Broadway, New York, NY 10001

National Investment Library, 32 Union Square, New York, NY 10003

National Investor Relations Institute, 2000 L St., N.W., Washington, DC, 20036

National Machine Tool Builders Association, 7901 Westpark Dr., McLean, VA 22102-4269

National OTC Stock Journal, PO Box 24327, Suite 400, 1780 S. Bellaire, Denver, CO 80222

National Partnership Exchange, PO Box 578, Tampa, FL 33601

National Quotation Bureau, 116 Nassau St., New York, NY 10038, tele. 1-212/765-7228

Nation's Business, 1615 H St., N.W., Washington, DC 20062

"Nation's Business Today," see ESPN

New Classics Library, Inc., PO Box 1618, Gainesville, GA 30503

New Issues, see Institute for Econometric Research

Newsday, Long Island, NY 11747

Newsletter Digest, 2201 Big Cove Rd., Huntsville, AL 35801

Newsletter Management Corp., American Media Group, 951 Broken Sound Pkwy., Baton Raton, FL 33431

News Letter on Newsletters, 44 W. Market St., Rhinebeck, NY 12572

New York Daily News, 220 E. 42nd St., New York, NY 10017

New York Futures Exchange, 20 Broad St., New York, NY 10005

New York Institute of Finance, 2 Broadway, 5th floor, New York, NY 10004

New York Mercantile Exchange, 4 World Trade Center, New York, NY 10048

New York Stock Exchange, 11 Wall St., New York, NY 10005

New York Times, 229 43rd St., New York, NY 10036

Ney (Richard) & Associates Asset Management, Box 90215, Pasadena, CA 91109

Nicholson Report, PO Box 56-1065, Miami, FL 33256

No-Load Fund Investor, PO Box 283, Hastings-on-Hudson, NY 10706

No-Load Fund X, 235 Montgomery St., San Francisco, CA, 94104

No-Load Mutual Fund Association, see Mutual Fund Education Alliance

No-Load Portfolios, 527 Hotel Plaza, Boulder City, NV 89005

North American Securities Administrators Association, 1-202/737-0900

Northern Miner, Northern Miner Press Ltd., 7 Labatt Ave., Toronto, Ontario M5A 3PZ, Canada

Norton (W.W.) Co., Inc., 500 Fifth Ave., New York, NY 10110

Oakley's Aggressive Stock Alert, see American Media Group

Oil & Gas Stocks Handbook, see Standard & Poor's

Olde Discount Corp., 751 Griswold St., Detroit, MI 48226

Omega Research, Inc., 3900 N.W. 79 Avenue, Suite 520, Miami, FL 33166

Option Advisor, Investment Research Institute, Inc., PO Box 46709, Cincinnati, OH 45246

Option Trader, 119 W. 57th St., New York, NY 10019

Options Clearing Corp., 440 S. LaSalle, Suite 908, Chicago, IL 60605

Options Handbook, see Standard & Poor's

Organization for Economic Co-operation and Development, 2001 L Street N.W., Suite 700, Washington, DC 20036

OTC Chart Manual, see Standard & Poor's

O.T.C. Growth Stock Watch, PO Box 305, Brookline, MA 02146

OTC Handbook, see Standard & Poor's

OTC Industrial Manual & News Reports, see Moody's

OTC Insight, Insight Capital Management, Inc., PO Box 127, Moraga, CA 94556

OTC Penny Stock Digest, Chis S. Metos, publisher, Boston Bldg., Nine Exchange Place, Salt Lake City, UT 84111

OTC Review and *OTC Review Special Situations*, OTC Review Inc., 37 E. 28th St., Suite 706, New York, NY 10016

Outlook (The), see Standard & Poor's

Outside Analyst, International Investment Publications, PO Box 70322, 1007 KH Amsterdam, The Netherlands

Pacific Stock Exchange, 301 Pine St., San Francisco, CA 94104

PaineWebber Group, Inc., 1285 Avenue of the Americas, New York, NY 10019

Paris Report (Alexander), 18-1 East Dundee Rd., Suite 110, Barrington, IL 60010

PC Computing, 4 Cambridge Center, Cambridge, MA 02142

Penny Mining Stock Report, PO Box 1217, Lafayette, CA 94549

Penny Stock News, now *Gold Mining Stock Report,* PO Box 1217, Lafa-yette, CA 94549

Penny Stock Preview, Idea Publishing Corp., 55 E. Afton Ave., Yardley, PA 19067

Penny Stock Venture, see Money Growth Institute

Personal Computing Magazine, VNU Business Publications, Inc., Ten Holland Dr., Hasbrouck Heights, NJ 07604

Personal Finance, see KCI Communications

Personal Investing News, Personal Investing News Corp., 951 Broken Sound Parkway, Boca Raton, FL 33431

Personal Investor, Plaza Communications, 18818 Teller Avenue, Suite 280, Irvine, CA 92715

Personal Portfolio Manager, PO Box 439, Purdys, NY 10578

Personal Wealth Reporter (for Canadian stocks) see Marpep

Petzold On The Market, 4455 Torrance, Blvd., Torrance, CA 90503

Philadelphia Stock Exchange, Philadelphia Board of Trade, 1900 Market St., Philadelphia, PA 19103

Phillips Publishing, Inc., 7811 Montrose Rd., Potomac, MD 20854

Pink Sheets, see National Quotation Bureau

Plain Talk Investor, 3310 Commercial Ave., Northbrook, IL 60062, tele. 1-708/564-1955

Portfolio Letter, Institutional Investor, 488 Madison Ave., New York, NY 10022

Portfolio Reports, 44 E. 4th St., New York, NY 10012

Praeger Publishers, One Madison Ave., New York, NY 10010

Predictions, Euler Enterprises, Suite 1200, 7910 Woodmont Ave., Bethesda, MD 20814

Prentice-Hall, Inc., Information Services Div., Paramus, NY 07652

Prescott, Ball & Turben, Inc., 1331 Euclid Ave., Cleveland, OH 44115

Primary Trend, 700 N. Water St., Milwaukee, WI 53202

Princeton Portfolios, 301 N. Harrison, Suite 229, Princeton, NJ 08540

Pring Market Review, 110 Blackville Rd., Washington Depot, CT 06794

Probus Publishing Co., 118 N. Clinton, Chicago, IL 60606

Prodigy, Prodigy Services Co., PO Box 4064, Woburn, MA 01888-9961

Professional Coin Grading Service, PO Box 9458, Newport Beach, CA 92658

Professional Investor (The), Lynatrace, Inc., 2593 S.E. 9th St., Pompano Beach, FL 33062

Professional Tape Reader, PO Box 2407, Hollywood, FL 33022

Profitable Investing, see Phillips Publishing

Prudent Market Decisions, 4 Cortland Ln., Greenville, RI 02828

Prudent Speculator (The), PO Box 1767, Santa Monica, CA 90406

Prudential-Bache Securities Inc., 100 Gold Street, New York, NY 10292

Public Service Broadcasting (PBS), 1320 Braddock Pl., Alexandria, VA 22314-1698

Public Utility Manual & News Reports, see Moody's

Puetz Investment Report (The), Division & 100 East, Fowler, IN 47944

Quick & Reilly, 120 Wall St., New York, NY 10005

Quotron, Quotron Systems, 12731 W. Jefferson Blvd., Los Angeles, CA 90066

Rating the Stock Selectors, 8949 La Riviera Drive, Sacramento, CA 95826

Real Estate Investor's Monthly, 342 Bryan Dr., Danville, CA 94526

Register of Corporations, Directors and Executives, see Standard & Poor's

Remnant Review, American Bureau of Economic Research, PO Box 8204, Fort Worth, TX 76124

Resource Recycling, Resource Recycling, Inc., Box 10540, Portland, OR 97210

Retirement Letter (The), see Phillips Publishing

Reuters Holdings, Reuters Ltd., 1700 Broadway, New York, NY 10019

Review of Securities Regulation, see Standard & Poor's

Ruff Times (The), Target Inc., 6612 Owens Dr., Pleasanton, CA 94566

Salomon Inc., One New York Plaza, New York, NY 10004

San Francisco Chronicle, 925 Mission St., San Francisco, CA 94103

Schultz (Harry) Letter, see *International Harry Schultz Letter*

Schwab (Charles), Investors Information Services, 101 Montgomery St., San Francisco, CA 94104

Scott Letter (The), Cole Publications, PO Box K-132, Richmond, VA 23288

Seattle Business, Vernon Publications, Suite 200, 3000 Northup Way, Bellevue, WA 98004

SEC News Digest, see Securities & Exchange Commission

SEC Today, see Commerce Clearing House

Sector Fund Connection, 8949 La Riviera Dr., Sacramento, CA 95826

Sector Funds Newsletter, PO Box 1210, Escondido, CA 92025

Securities and Exchange Commission, 450 5th St. N.W., Washington, DC 20549, tele. 1-202/272-7450

Securities Industry Association, 120 Broadway, 35th Floor, New York, NY 10271

Securities Research Co., 208 Newbury St., Boston, MA 02116

Securities Traders' Monthly, Dealers' Digest, Inc., 2 World Trade Center, New York, NY 10048

Securities Week, McGraw-Hill Publications, 1221 Avenue of the Americas, New York, NY 10020

Security Analysis (Benjamin Graham-David L. Dodd), see McGraw-Hill, tele. 1-212/512-2000

Security Dealers of North America, see Standard & Poor's

Select Information Exchange, 2095 Broadway, New York, NY 10023

Seminars International, Inc., 951 Broken Sound Pkwy, NW. PO Box 3079, Boca Raton, FL 33431-0979

Shearson Lehman Hutton, American Express Tower, World Financial Center, 200 Vesey St., New York, NY 10285

Short Alert, see WMP Enterprises

Sinclair Commentary, PO Box 27, Amenia, NY 12501

Smart Money, Hirsch Organization, 6 Deer Trail, Old Tappan, NJ 07675

Smartvest, 751 Griswold St., Detroit, MI 48226

Smith Barney, Harris Upham & Co., 1345 Avenue of the Americas, New York, 10105

Sound Advice, 191 N. Hartz Ave., Suite 6, Danville, CA 94526

Source Information Network, Source Telecomputing Corp., 1616 Anderson Rd., McLean, VA 22102

Special Situation Report, PO Box 167, Rochester, NY 14601

Special Situations Newsletter, C.H. Kaplan Research Associates, 150 Nassau St., Room 1926, New York, NY 10038

Speculator (The), Growth in Funds, Inc., 77 S. Palm Ave., Sarasota, FL 34236

Springfield Report (The), PO Box 833, Henderson, NV 89015

Standard & Poor's, 25 Broadway, New York, NY 10004

Statistical Service, see Standard & Poor's

Staton's Stock Market Advisory, 300 E. Boulevard, B-4, Charlotte, NC 28203

Stephens (E. David), 1-800/421-0190

Stock Guide, see Standard & Poor's

Stock Market Cycles, 2260 Cahuenga Blvd., #305, Los Angeles, CA 90068

Stock Market Encyclopedia, see Standard & Poor's

Stock Market Magazine, 16 School St., Yonkers, NY 10701

Stock Market Monitor, PO Box 403, Naperville, IL 60566

Stock Reports, see Standard & Poor's

Stock Summary, see Standard & Poor's

Stockbroker, 4311 Wilshire Blvd., Los Angeles, CA 90010

Strategic Investment, 824 E. Baltimore St., Baltimore, Md., 21202

Strategy Simulator (The), William Finnegan Associates, Inc., PO Box 1121, Malibu, CA 90265

Survey of Current Business, Public Information Office, Bureau of Economic Analysis, Department of Commerce, Washington, DC 20230

Survey of Wall Street Research, Find/SVP, 625 Avenue of the Americas, New York, NY 10011

Swingtrend, 120 E. 56th St., New York, NY 10022

Switch Fund Timing, PO Box 25430, Rochester, NY 14625

Systems & Forecasts, Signalert Corp., 150 Great Neck Rd., Great Neck, NY 11021

System Writer Plus, see Omega Research

Tabell's Market Letter, 600 Alexander Rd., Princeton, NJ 08540

Taipan, 824 E. Baltimore St., Baltimore, MD 21202

Target, Inc., PO Box 25, Pleasanton, CA 94566

Tax Hotline, 330 W. 42nd St., New York, NY 10036

Technical Analysis of Stocks & Commodities, Stocks & Commodities Magazine

Technical Trends, Merrill Analaysis, Inc., PO Box 792, Dept. B914, Wilton, CT 06897

Telephone Switch Newsletter, PO Box 2538, Huntington Beach, CA 92647, tele. 1-800/950-8765

Telerate Systems, Inc., One World Trade Center, New York, NY 10048

Telescan, Telescan Inc., 2900 Wilcrest, Houston, TX 77042, tele. 1-800/727-4636

"This Morning's Business," see Financial News Network

Time Warner Inc., Time & Life Building, Rockefeller Center, New York, NY 10020

Timer Digest, PO Box 1688 Greenwich, CT 06836, tele. 1-800/356-2527

TJFR, Business News Reporter, TJFR Publishing Co., Inc., Suite #1105, 82 Wall Street, New York, NY 10005

Top Trader Insight, PO Box 7634, Beverly Hills, CA 90212-7634

Traders Hotline, Zweig Securities Advisory Service, Inc., 900 3rd Ave., New York, NY 10022

Transmarket Group, tele. 1-800/362-8117

Transportation Manual & News Reports, see Moody's

Trendline Stock Charts, see Standard & Poor's

Turner Communications Co., Inc., 1018 E. Peachtree St. N.E., Atlanta, GA 30309

United & Babson Investment Report and *United Mutual Fund Selector*, 101 Prescott St., Wellesly Hills, MA 02181

Unit Investment Trusts, see Standard & Poor's

United States Government, (see, Bureau of Economic Analysis, Bureau of the Census, Department of Commerce, Department of Energy, Department of the Treasury, Federal Trade Commission, Federal Reserve System, International Trade Administration and Securities & Exchange Commission. For addresses of other government offices see *The United States Government Manual* available at most libraries.)

USA Today, Gannett Co., PO Box 7858, Washington, DC 20044

U.S. News & World Report, Subscription Dept., PO Box 55929, Boulder, CO 80322-5929

Utility Forecaster (The), see KCI Communications

Value Line, Inc. 711 Third Ave., New York, NY 10017

Vanderbilt University, Nashville, TN 37235

Vickers Stock Traders Guide, Vickers Associates, Inc., 226 New York Ave., Huntington, NY 11743

Vickers Stock Research Corp., Box 59, Brookside, NJ 07926

Video Course on Technical Analysis, see International Institute for Technical Research

Virginia Commonwealth University, Richmond, VA 23284

Volume Reversal Survey (The), Box 1451, Sedona, AZ 86336

Wall Street Astrologer, Mull Publishing, Box 11133, Indianapolis, IN 46201

Wall Street Computer Review magazine, 150 Broadway, New York, NY 10038

"Wall Street Computer Review" television show, see Financial News Network

Wall Street Digest (The), 214 Carnegie Ctr., Princeton, NJ 08540

Wall Street Generalist, MarketMetrics, Inc.(cq), Suite 6, 1266 First St., Sarasota, FL 33577

Wall Street Journal, see Dow Jones & Co.

Wall Street Reports, 120 Wall St., New York, NY 10005

Wall Street Review of Books, Redgrave Publishing Co., 380 Adams St., Bedford Hills, NY 10507

Wall Street Transcript, 99 Wall St., New York, NY 10005

Wall Street Week, Owens Mills, MD 21117

Warner Computer Systems, One University Place, Hackensack, NJ 07601

Washington Post (The), 1150 15th St., N.W., Washington, DC 20071

Wealth Monitors, 1001 East 101st Terrace, Suite 200, Kansas City, MO 64131

Weber's Fund Advisor, PO Box 3490, New Hyde Park, NY 11040

Weekly Fund Advisor, 1-800/346-0138

Weiss Research, Inc., P.O. Box 2923, West Palm Beach, FL 33402

Wellington Letter, 733 Bishop St., Honolulu, HI 96813

Wellington's Worry-Free Investing, c/o Euler Enterprises, Inc., 7910 Woodmont Ave., Suite 1200, Bethesda, MD 20814

Western Investor, Willamette Publishing, Inc., Suite 1115, 400 SW 6th Ave., Portland, OR 97204

WFI Corp., 357 S. Robertson Blvd., Beverly Hills, CA 90211

Wiley (John) & Sons, 605 Third Ave., New York, NY 10158

WMP Enterprises, 3443 Parkway Center Court, Orlando, FL 32808

Wolanchuk Report, 1-900/234-7777 ext. 69 ($2 per minute)

World Coin News, Krause Publications, 700 E. State St., Iola, WI 54990

World Perspective Communications, 3443 Parkway Center Court, Orlando, FL 32808

Young's Intelligence Report, see Phillips Publishing tele. 1-800/722-9000

Young's International Gold Report, see Phillips Publishing

Young's World Money Forecast, Young Research & Publishing, Inc., Federal Bldg., Thames St., Newport, RI 02840

Your Money, see Cable News Network

Your Window Into The Future, c/o Moneypower, PO Box 22586, Minneapolis, MN 55422

Zweig Forecast (The), PO Box 360, Bellmore, NY 11710

Zweig Performance Ratings Report, PO Box 360, Bellmore, NY 11710

Zaner & Co., Futures Discount Group, tele. 1-800/872-6673

Index